D0548281

Powys

37218 00503652 5

For my darlin' Dick. Aren't we clever? Our magical family journey starts here and I can't wait for our beautiful son, Arthur Donald Strawbridge, to find out how wonderful, kind and inspiring his Daddy is.

the VINTAGE SWEETS book

Angel Adoree

MITCHELL BEAZLEY

LLYFRGELLOEDD POWYS LIBRARIES

ILLUSTRATIONS by ADELE MILDRED

the VINTAGE SWEETS book
by Angel Adoree

First published in Great Britain in 2013 by Mitchell Beazley, an imprint of Octopus Publishing Group Limited,
Endeavour House, 189 Shaftesbury Avenue, London WC2H 8JY
www.octopusbooks.co.uk

An Hachette UK Company
www.hachette.co.uk

Copyright © Octopus Publishing Group Limited 2013 | Text copyright © Angel Adoree 2013

Publishers' notes Although the advice and information in this book are believed to be accurate and true at the time of going to press, neither the author nor the publishers can accept any legal responsibility or liability for any errors or omissions that may have been made, nor for any inaccuracies nor for any loss, harm or injury that comes about from following instructions or advice in this book.

This book contains some dishes made with raw or lightly cooked eggs. It is prudent for more vulnerable people, such as pregnant and nursing mothers, people with weakened immune systems, the elderly, babies, and young children, to avoid dishes made with uncooked or lightly cooked eggs.

The prep time listed for each recipe represents the amount of time it takes to complete all stages of the recipe prior to cooking. The total time includes the prep time.

All rights reserved. Except where instructed, no part of this work may be reproduced or utilized in any form or by any means, electronic or mechanical, including photocopying, recording, or by any information storage and retrieval system, without the prior written permission of the publishers.

The author has asserted her moral rights.

ISBN: 978 1 84533 832 9 (large format) | 978 1 84533 831 2 (small format)

Set in Reminga, Gorey, Justlefthand, and Lady Rene.

Printed and bound in China.

Commissioning Editor **Eleanor Maxfield** | Deputy Art Director & Designer **Yasia Williams-Leedham** | Senior Editor **Leanne Bryan**
Creative Director **Angel Adoree** | Photographers **Yuki Sugiura** (food & drink); **David Edwards** (projects & locations) | Illustrator **Adele Mildred**
Food Stylist **Miranda Keyes** | Head of Craft **Sarah Keen** | Copy Editor **Salima Hirani** | Proofreader **Emma Callery**
Indexer **Cathy Heath** | Assistant Production Manager **Caroline Alberti**

Sweet beginnings 20

I always like to kill two birds with one stone so, in this chapter, I teach you all the basics of sweetie-making while taking you on a trip down memory lane. You'll learn to make Love Hearts for your sweetheart, Parma Violets for your gran, Fruit Jellies for your friends, Sugared Mice for the kids, Jazzies for a party and a couple of naughty, sweetie-inspired cocktails for yourself!

Softball, firmball & hardball sweets 54

Who was the first to discover that some beautiful alchemy takes place when you heat up sugar in a bit of water? Well, whoever they were, I hope they are luxuriating in heaven as we speak! And you will be too when you suck on the spoils of this chapter –Toffee Bonbons, Liquorice, Gumdrops, Marshmallows, Rum & Raisin Fudge, Edinburgh Rock and other glorious delights.

Soft-crack & hard-crack sweets 90

Do you find it impossible to resist crunching on a firm sweet? Or do you have the self-discipline to keep sucking? Either way, the sugar thermometer will be your new best friend as you learn to take sugar up to molten temperatures to create your favourite hard sweeties of yesteryear – Toffee, Nut Brittle, Rhubarb & Custard Sweets, Rock, Sherbet Dips – all the old favourites are here!

INTRODUCTION

Welcome to *The Vintage Sweets Book*. You are about to embark on a nostalgic journey and rediscover your childhood fascination with all things sweet. The following pages show you how, with a 'spoonful of sugar' and a little imagination, you can create your favourite vintage sweets and party treats.

This book is divided into three chapters representing the techniques used in transforming humble sugar into something marvellous and magical. Chapter 1, Sweet Beginnings, is, as the name implies, the perfect place to start if you are new to making sweets. This chapter is full of your old favourites but the recipes do not require advanced skills or even a sugar thermometer! Chapter 2, Softball, Firmball & Hardball Sweets, is for when your confidence has built a little and you have the taste for the sweet life. This chapter allows you to explore what happens once sugar is heated. It requires some practice and patience, but is so much fun for the whole family. (Of course it's obvious, but let me say it anyway – hot sugar can be dangerous, so please take great care and never leave a pan unattended!) Chapter 3, Soft-Crack & Hard-Crack Sweets, is for the confident sugar thermometer user. The techniques in this chapter allow you to produce sweeties that you may never have thought possible. You will also learn how to pull sugar, and are very likely to get addicted to this exciting technique!

Along with the recipes and skills required to create your sweet childhood favourites, I offer some quirky packaging ideas and share with you my finest tips for throwing the best Sweet-Tea Party ever!

My Journey

I like old things. Unique one-off items with character and charm excite me. Old-fashioned rituals, manners and ways of life define me. I live and breathe a past time when life was simpler, yet steeped in sweet elegance.

I discovered my passion for all things vintage when I was only a few years old. My family is from the East End of London and I was brought up by ladies that I considered to be the most beautiful and elegant in all the land!

My family is very open-hearted and my parents were always throwing soirées when I was younger. They now spend their days running a wonderful restaurant and making people smile on a daily basis. We have always worked hard as a family, but we know the importance of family time and this always revolves around food! My early experiences – shared with them around the dining table, at the kitchen

Left: Mum and dad as teenagers, 1966.

counter and on many a picnic blanket – are the source of my passion for entertaining.

During my teens, I started thrifting at a local car boot sale and became addicted to hunting down glamorous old items. I would buy clothes that did not fit, tea sets I would not use and a variety of other items that cluttered up my room and sent my parents into a spin!

In my early 20s, I finally made my addiction into my first business, called the Angel-A Vintage Experience. I would sell my finds while spoiling my guests with wonderful food and drink.

Hosting is part of my being and, in 2007, my humble beginnings in vintage hospitality took the natural progression into a fully-fledged vintage hospitality business. The Vintage Patisserie was born, offering bespoke vintage parties. I have to pinch myself every day that I get to bring the glorious visions of entertaining that my clients have into fruition, and make important events such as hen parties, weddings, christenings and birthdays the special occasions that they should be. I make many people smile and this fact fills my heart with happiness each time I remember it!

In 2010, I was blessed with the opportunity to write *The Vintage Tea Party Book*, in which I was allowed to share

Top: My Great Grandparents, Nan and her twin sister (my Great Aunt) – at the seaside, 1927.

Bottom: My Dad (far right) with my Nan and their friends in Victoria Park, London, 1956.

my passion for food and drink on pages that I could style with my vintage finds. The book was very well received and, in 2012, I launched *The Vintage Tea Party Year Book*, which celebrates all the special occasions that one calendar year provides – I will take up any opportunity to host a party!

That was a year of relentless hard work for me and it was also a very special year for us Brits. The Diamond Jubilee and the London 2012 Olympic Games filled me with patriotic pride and I had the honour of hosting the Women's Institute tent at the Thames Diamond Jubilee Pageant.

THE PRESENT

I've had an incredible, life-changing year and hosted most events with a bump that grew into my son Arthur Donald Strawbridge.

The Vintage Patisserie has had its one-year anniversary at its new home in Hackney, East London, and has been growing from strength to strength, hosting events, hair and hospitality academies… and even taxidermy classes! Already the walls are bursting with stories from parties and my team has done me proud by taking over the events and letting me have some down time to be a mum.

I've never had down time before – learning how to take it is something I've had to teach myself. I've learned to 'smell the roses', some may say! I've had time to fall in love with my little boy and grow my family life. Time is a wonderful medium, especially when you have had so little of it before, and I have spent the past year thinking of my childhood and quizzing my parents and grandparents on everything possible. Your early years define you and one subject came up again and again – sweets.

The Sweet Years

I never realised until now that I could map my early life with sweets. Unlike any other food, they tell a tale on their own. Sweets were my first investment. At the tender age of five, when I received my first 20 pence pocket money, I had a wealth of choices! Do I start to save? Do I buy a magazine? Do I buy a cake? No, there was only one real choice – I went to buy sweets.

Why? Well, I'm five years old, I enter my local sweetie shop and there is jar after jar of jewelled sweets in every colour, shape and size imaginable, each with its own flavour and particular sensation. With my 20 pence, I can fill a whole bag and have at least a day's worth of enjoyment from it. I can even give some sweets to my brother and my friends and still have enough for me! Why would I choose to buy anything else?

Every Saturday when I received my 20 pence, I would walk down the road by myself and spend hours choosing. I was not the only child there – the sweet shop was a meeting place for my school friends that was almost completely free of adult supervision.

My Nan worked in one of the most famous sweetie shops in the City of London during my very early years. Every time we saw her she would bring us a different sweet, and I can honestly say I don't remember receiving the same sweet twice over a span of years. I blame Nan for my sweet tooth and the start of my love affair with sugar!

Top: Meeting a queen on Daybreak TV for the Diamond Jubilee, June 2012.
Middle: Launch of The Vintage Tea Party Year Book, September 2012.
Bottom: Family photo, March 2013.

Funfairs filled with candy floss, theme parks filled with fudge, Grandma's suitcase filled with Turkish delight, Nan's drawers filled with nougat, seaside shops full of rock, school playgrounds full of Love Hearts – yes, I can map my life with sweets and I'm excited that my son will do the same. In fact, we as a family may even do it together (during his younger years, anyway!).

YOUR JOURNEY

The importance of sweets throughout childhood, sprinkled with family life and a love of giving, has inspired the pages ahead of you.

Watching sugar develop through its stages of cooking is an enchanting and thrilling experience. Getting the whole family involved will be a given – watch Dad get all geeky with the technicalities of the hard-crack sweets and the pulling of sugar. When we make ours, my partner Dick does the physical jobs and he loves it!

With this in mind, I've added a few cocktails with sweet inspiration, so when it becomes grown-up o'clock, you can use your sweet makings of the day for some delicious refreshments!

You will quickly learn that the sweets you make are like nothing you can buy in the shops. Fresh sweets will become your secret weapon in wooing! And the possibilities are really endless. I've added as many techniques as possible to the pages, but it's up to you to be creative with each recipe and add flavour and colour twists.

For the cost of a bag of sugar, and with some elbow grease, you now have the tools to make sweets and treats for your family, along with gifts for special occasions (perhaps wedding favours?) and parties. And, as a firm believer in the phrase 'the first bite is with the eye', I've included some beautifully hand-illustrated packaging ideas for you to present your sweet jewels in, too – templates for these can be downloaded from my website (vintagepatisserie.co.uk), allowing you to print out and make up some delightful containers for your homemade sweeties with wonderful results that defy the ease of making them!

With all your new skills for making sweeties, cocktails and party treats, it would be a crime to not hold a Sweet-Tea Party! Fill your family and friends with love and warmth adorned in vintage style and take them on your sweet journey with you. On pages 10–13 you will find some ready-made invitations and thank-you notes. Feel free to photocopy them to use as your own, or download them from my website. On that note, I would like to thank you for reading this book and I raise my lollipop to you:

'To your perfect Sweet-Tea Party, whether it be one of simple family fun-time in the kitchen or of extending your sweet love to include all the sweetest people in your life.'

Angel aged 4, 1981.

Love Angel

Sweetie Know-How

Sweets are made from just sugar and water, yet the variety available is truly phenomenal. The transformation of these humble ingredients into sweets is a fascinating process. Although it may seem complex to the uninitiated, making sweets is not difficult. To understand the basics, you need to know what happens when sugar syrup – a mixture of sugar and water – is heated to various temperatures.

Very simply, when sugar syrup is heated, the water content boils away, so the mixture becomes more sugary (ie the sugar concentration increases). Water by itself can only reach 100°C (212°F) when heated, as the water turns to steam and evaporates at this temperature. But with sugar in the mix, much higher temperatures can be reached and it is the height of the temperature that determines the character of the sugar syrup when it has cooled down.

For example, at 112–116°C (234–240°F), the syrup is at the softball stage. You may not be surprised to read that if you take a bit of the syrup that is at this temperature from the bubbling pan and drop it into cold water (to cool it down), it will form a 'soft ball' that you can squeeze between your fingers. This is the ideal texture for fudge, among other sweets. As you cook a sugar syrup to higher temperatures, it will go through various stages, each of which produces sweeties of a different texture. Generally speaking, the higher the temperature reached, the greater the sugar concentration is and the harder and more brittle the texture of the cooled sweet will be. Most of the recipes in this book will tell you to boil your sugar mixture until it reaches one of the stages outlined below.

Sugar temperatures, stages and characteristics

The thread stage
When the temperature of the sugar syrup reaches 110–111°C (230–232°F), it has reached the thread stage and has a sugar concentration of 80 per cent. When you drop a little of this syrup into cold water, it forms a liquid thread that will not ball up. Cooking sugar syrup to this stage gives you not sweets but syrup – something you might make to pour over ice cream, for instance.

The softball stage
At 112–116°C (234–240°F), sugar syrup reaches the softball stage, with a sugar concentration of 85 per cent. At this temperature, sugar syrup dropped into cold water will form a soft, flexible ball. If you remove the ball from the water, it will flatten like a pancake after a few moments in your hand. This is the stage to stop cooking a sugar syrup if you are making fudge, pralines or fondant.

THE SWEETIE-MAKING STAGES

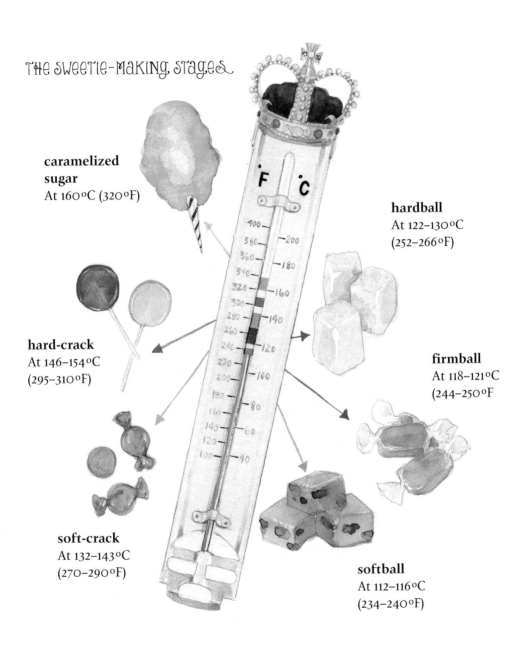

caramelized sugar
At 160°C (320°F)

hardball
At 122–130°C (252–266°F)

hard-crack
At 146–154°C (295–310°F)

firmball
At 118–121°C (244–250°F

soft-crack
At 132–143°C (270–290°F)

softball
At 112–116°C (234–240°F)

The firmball stage

At 118–121°C (244–250°F), a sugar syrup has reached the firmball stage and has a sugar concentration of 87 per cent. Drop a little of this syrup in cold water and it will form a firm ball, one that won't flatten when you take it out of the water, but instead remains malleable. It will flatten when squeezed. Caramels are cooked to the firmball stage.

The hardball stage

At 122–130°C (252–266°F), the sugar syrup has reached the hardball stage. The syrup forms thick, 'ropey' threads as it drips from the spoon. The sugar concentration is rather high now (92 per cent), which means it contains less and less moisture. A little of this syrup dropped into cold water will form a hard ball. If you take the ball out of the water, it won't flatten. The ball will be hard, but you can still change its shape by squashing it. Nougat and marshmallows are cooked to the hardball stage.

The soft-crack stage

At 132–143°C (270–290°F), the syrup has reached the soft-crack stage and has a sugar concentration of 95 per cent and a very low moisture content. As the syrup reaches this stage, the bubbles on top will become smaller, thicker and closer together. When you drop a bit of this syrup into cold water, it will solidify into threads that, when removed from the water, are flexible, not brittle. They will bend slightly before breaking. Taffy and butterscotch are cooked to the soft-crack stage.

The hard-crack stage

At 146–154°C (295–310°F), the sugar syrup has reached the hard-crack stage and has a sugar concentration of 99 per cent. The hard-crack stage is the highest temperature you are likely to see specified in a sweetie recipe. At these temperatures, there is almost no water left in the syrup. Drop a little of the molten syrup into cold water and it will form hard, brittle threads that break when bent. Toffee, nut brittles and lollipops are all cooked to the hard-crack stage.

USEFUL TECHNIQUES

You'll find the following techniques will come in handy as you work through the recipes in this book.

Caramelizing sugar

If you heat a sugar syrup to temperatures higher than 160°C (320°F), you will boil away all the water content and end up with a product that has a 100 per cent sugar concentration – and you will have created caramelized sugar. Candy floss is made from sugar syrup heated to this temperature. As the temperature rises, caramelized sugar will pass through the three following stages:

- LIGHT AMBER IN COLOUR – at this stage the sugar is ideal for making toffee apples or to use for garnishes.

- BROWN IN COLOUR – at this stage, the sugar begins to break down and has a rich, complex flavour and is perfect for making sugar baskets and basket spirals.

- BURNT SUGAR – if the temperature rises above 180°C (356°F), the sugar burns and becomes bitter. Throw it out if it reaches this stage!

Removing sugar crystals

In a good few of the recipes, you'll be instructed to remove the sugar crystals from the inside of the pan. As a sugar syrup is heating, sugar crystals form on the inside of the pan, above the bubbling solution. It's important to remove these because, if you don't, the crystals will affect the texture and structure of your sweets. Instead of being smooth and a pleasure to suck, they will become grainy.

Removing sugar crystals is very simple to do: simply put a lid on the pan once the solution starts to boil and keep it in place for 3 minutes. The steam will condense and run down the insides of the pan, taking the sugar crystals with it. When you take off the lid, you can then remove any stubborn crystals by wiping the inside of the pan with a pastry brush dipped in warm water.

Creating your own sweet moulds

For many of the recipes in this book you will need a sweet mould. You can easily source silicone sweet moulds of every shape and size online. A cheaper option is to make your own. To do so, pack sifted icing sugar approximately 2.5cm (1in) deep into a large plastic container. Tamp down the sugar, but not too firmly. Next, make impressions in the icing sugar in the shape required for your sweets.

- • TO MAKE CUBIC MOULDS – push a small cube-shaped object that's about 1.2 × 1.2cm (½ × ½in) and about 1.2cm (½in) deep into the icing sugar. Make your next impression about 2.5cm (1in) along. Repeat until you have the required number of moulds.

- • TO MAKE HEMISPHERICAL MOULDS – push a marble taped on to a fork into the icing sugar. Make your next impression about 2.5cm (1in) along. Repeat until you have the required number of moulds. (To make spherical sweets, make the sweet halves in two batches, popping one of the hemispheres from the first batch on top of one of the hemispheres in the second batch when the second batch is in the moulds but still slightly liquid.)

Personalizing your sweets

To inscribe your sweets with letters or messages – perhaps heartfelt notes to your loved one – you can use edible markers to write on each sweetie (using a letter stencil, if you like) once it is completely dry. If you wish to go the extra mile, why not order a text embossing set (*see* Resources, page 154) and stamp messages on to your sweets using a small paintbrush and a little food colouring of your choice? Alternatively, you can emboss softer sweets – such as Liquorice (*see* pages 76–7) with a homemade stamp to give them that personal touch.

Filling sweet moulds

The easiest way to fill sweet moulds is to use a piston funnel. However, as these are expensive, you might like to make your own by pushing the handle of a wooden spoon down into the neck of an ordinary funnel. You then fill the funnel with your sugary mixture and ease the wooden spoon in and out to allow a controlled flow of the liquid into the moulds.

Alternative methods for filling sweet moulds include spooning the sugar syrup into the moulds, or pouring it in carefully using a Pyrex jug – but be wary of drips.

Pulling sugar

It is essential to master this technique in order to make the soft- and hard-crack sweets in the third chapter of this book. To do so, pour sugar syrup that has reached the correct temperature on to a silicone mat. Using a scraper, repeatedly fold the edges of the syrup into the centre, working around the edges until the mixture is cool enough to handle. Then lift the syrup off the mat and roll it into a cylinder. Take hold of the mass with both hands and stretch it apart until it forms a long rope. Bring the ends back together again, creating a 'U' shape, twist the two halves together, then roll into a cylinder again. Continue to pull, bend, twist and roll the sugar for about 10–15 minutes until the mixture starts to become creamy and satiny. If the sugar becomes too difficult to work with, warm it on a prepared tray in the oven for 5 minutes, or place it under a heat lamp until it softens. Once the sugar has reached the desired consistency, you can make your sweets, cutting and shaping as required.

USEFUL EQUIPMENT

Certain items are essential for sweet-making. Some of these you'll have knocking about your kitchen already, but in a few cases, a little investment is necessary to bring your sweetie dreams into fruition.

Sugar thermometer

This is the single most important piece of equipment used when making sweets. Unless you are an expert at working with sugar, using a sugar thermometer is the only way to know for sure if your sugar syrup has reached a certain temperature and, therefore, the stage you are after.

You should always test a new thermometer to ensure it is accurate before you set out on any candy-making adventures. Put your new sugar thermometer into a pan of water and bring it to the boil. The thermometer should then read 100 °C (212 °F). If it doesn't, agitate it slightly in its holder until it does! If it doesn't, gauge the difference between the actual temperature and the reading given by the thermometer and remember to make the necessary adjustment when using the thermometer during cooking.

When using your thermometer to test the temperature of hot sugar syrup, make sure you heat it under a hot tap first, because putting a cold thermometer into a very hot sugar mixture could cause it to crack. The same applies for cooling the thermometer. Leave it to cool naturally – do not put a sugar thermometer under cold water immediately after use in a hot pan. Ensure your thermometer does not touch the base of the pan, as it won't give an accurate reading.

Silicone mat

This nifty bit of kit is most useful when working with sugar at the soft- and hard-crack stage, as it provides the perfect surface on to which you can pour your hot sugar and work with it as it cools down.

Pans, baking sheets and silicone spatulas

These may already be part of your kitchen equipment collection, so hopefully there will be no need for you to go out and buy them when you first begin working with sugar. Cleaning sticky sugar residues off them can be tricky; to do so, soak in very hot water.

Moulds

While I do suggest the shape of moulds to use
for certain sweetie recipes (and list stockists
for these on page 154), the shapes you go for
are entirely down to your individual preference.
However, I would suggest that, whichever shapes
you plump for, you buy silicone moulds, as they can
take the heat of molten sugar and it is easy to remove
sweets from them.

Nonstick baking spray

Spraying this inside your silicone sweetie moulds before filling
them will make it easier to pop the sweets out of the mould once they're set, and also
helps to guard against sweets having uneven shapes or holes in them. Using baking spray in
sweetie-making is preferable to brushing moulds with oil as it is less time-consuming, and you
get a fine, even coverage.

OTHER POINTS TO REMEMBER

Colouring and flavouring

Just a quick flick through the pages in this book will reveal that sweeties can come in a dazzling
variety of colours and flavours, all achieved with the help of glorious food colourings and flavourings.
As with mould shapes, I give you my suggestions for which flavours and colours I think work well
for each recipe, but feel free to experiment and make these recipes your own. When flavourings and/
or colourings are used, I give in the ingredients list the total amount to be used within that recipe.
For example, if 20 drops are to be used, I might suggest you divide the mixture into 5 portions and use
4 drops of a different colour per portion. Take this as nothing more than a general guideline. Use 20
drops of one colour for the entire quantity, if you yearn for sweeties all of your favourite colour, or
divide the mixture into 20 portions and use 1 drop of a different colour per portion, if that is your
desire. It's entirely up to you! The same applies to flavouring quantities.

Specialist equipment and ingredients

If you rushed out to buy all the specialist sweetie-making equipment available at one fell swoop,
it would set you back a pretty penny. However, sweetie-making need not break the bank; a better
approach is to buy the equipment and ingredients you need piece by piece as you work your way
through the recipes in this book – most of which can be achieved with very little investment.
This means that over time, and without ever really feeling it in the pocket,
you'll end up with the best-stocked sweetie-making cupboard in town!

On page 154 you'll find a list of specialist items that are a not so easy
to get hold of (such as silicone rose-shaped lolly moulds, used to
make the Rose Lollipops on pages 134–5, or sarsaparilla root for
the Sarsaparilla Cocktail on pages 124–5) with stockists that you
can rely on, to help you build your marvellous collection.

SWEET BEGINNINGS

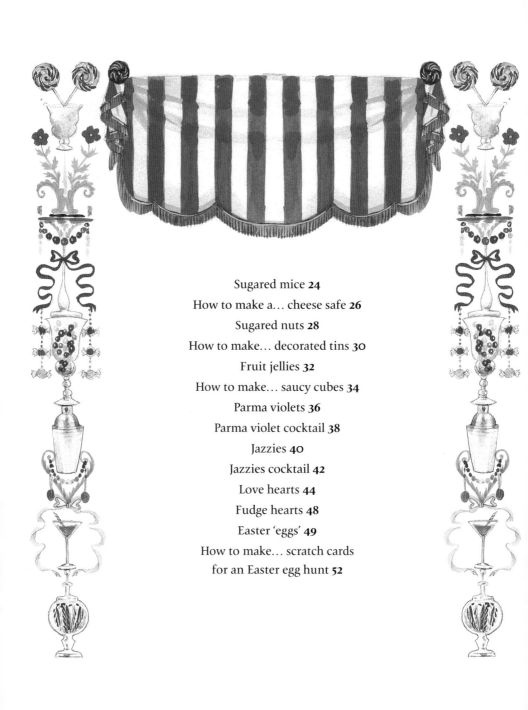

Welcome to the dating chapter! In these pages, you'll become rather intimate with sugar and begin to learn how it works as you transform humble bags of the sweet stuff into various sweets and get to grips with the fascinating culinary art of sweet-making.

You'll be happy to learn that many of your childhood favourites are included and delighted to discover how incredibly easy they are to make. Mould a few Sugared Mice with your children, eat some and give some as gifts. (And, while you're at it, make a Cheese Safe – to keep your cheese safe from the mice, of course!) Press a batch of Love Hearts or make tempting Fudge Hearts to express your undying love to someone special, or to woo someone that you would like to become special! Try making Sugared Nuts – my take on the famous sugared almonds – along with a beautifully illustrated tin (using artwork downloaded from my website) to give as the perfect wedding gift, made with love. Fancy Fruit Jellies for an after-dinner *petit four*? Or Parma Violets, to remind you of your granny? Then you're in the right chapter! Remember Jazzies? These could not be simpler to make and are great sticky fun! And if all that's not enough, you'll also find a few sweet cocktails and instructions for organizing a wonderful Easter egg hunt. Enjoy and get messy!

These cute treats traditionally found their place snuggling inside children's Christmas stockings. Nowadays, they can be bought in opulent outlets, looking stylish in exquisite packaging, with a price tag to match! For the cost of some icing sugar, eggs and elbow grease you can create a gift fit for any quirky personality. You can even package your mice in a beautiful homemade box (*see* pages 84–5).

PREP TIME:
10 minutes

TOTAL TIME:
30 minutes, plus
24 hours for drying

MAKES: 12

Sugared Mice

400g (14oz) icing sugar, plus extra for dusting
1 large free-range egg white
few drops of red or black food colouring (optional)
fine string, for the tails (optional)

1 Sieve the icing sugar into a large bowl. In a separate bowl, whisk the egg whites until they are frothy. Mix the egg whites into the icing sugar until a paste forms.

2 Dust your work surface with icing sugar, turn out the mixture on to the surface and knead it until it is smooth. If the dough is sticky, dust with more icing sugar. Add some food colouring, if liked, and knead it into the fondant. Alternatively, divide the fondant into portions to make mice of a number of different colours.

3 If you are using mouse-shaped jelly moulds, press the warm fondant into the ungreased moulds and smooth off the undersides. Add a small piece of string for the tail, if desired. Stand the filled moulds on a clean tray and leave the sugared mice to dry at room temperature or, preferably, in a cool room, for roughly 24 hours until they are completely firm. Remove the mice from the moulds and, using a cocktail stick, apply small drops of food colouring to give each mouse eyes and a nose, if liked.

4 If you don't have moulds, divide the fondant into 12 equal portions. Wrap the ones you are not handling in clingfilm so they don't dry out. To shape each mouse, pull off a small amount of fondant from 1 portion and shape the head. Use the remaining fondant to form an oval shape for the body, then press the head against the body while both are still soft enough to adhere. Add tails and decorate the head as before. Arrange the mice on a clean tray and leave to dry in the air for 24 hours.

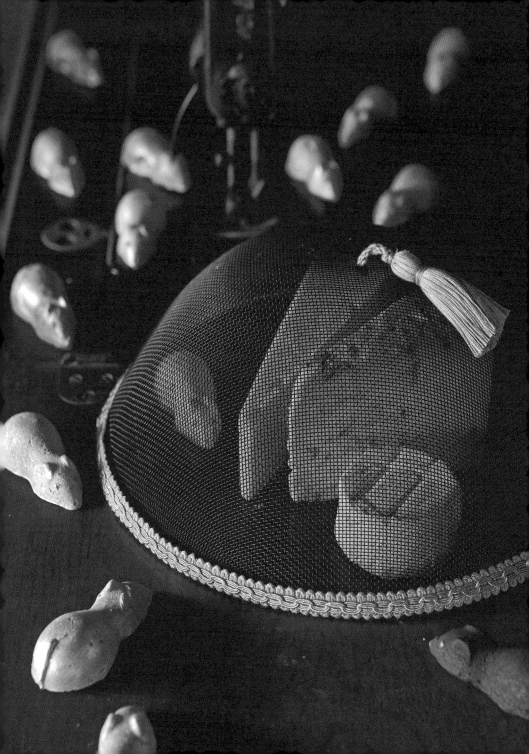

How to Make a
CHEESE SAFE

I wish I still thought mice were cute cheese-eating pets. As a child, I'm sure that I even left a piece of cheese out for them to take back to their house beyond the walls. Nowadays, I understand that cheese tastes best at room temperature and a great way to keep it from unwanted dinner guests is to cover it with a cheese safe (made with a sieve and as stylish as they come).

YOU WILL NEED

hacksaw ✂ sieve (metal or plastic – plastic is easier to cut) ✂
coarse sandpaper ✂ newspaper ✂ black spray paint (for metal or plastic,
as per your sieve) ✂ 50cm (½yd) gold trimming ✂ glue gun ✂
fabric scissors ✂ pencil ✂ 1 gold curtain tassel

1 Using the hacksaw, carefully remove the sieve's handle, then sand down any dangerous sharp edges on the area from which the handle has been removed with sandpaper. (You don't need to make it perfectly smooth, as this area will be covered with trimming later.)

2 In a well-ventilated area, lay out a few sheets of newspaper, then spray one side of your sieve with the black spray paint. Leave to dry, then turn it over and spray the other side. You may need to apply a couple of coats to each side to achieve an even covering.

3 Once the sieve is dry all over, attach the gold trimming around the rim of the sieve using the glue gun. Cut off any excess trimming.

4 Find the centre of your sieve and push the tip of a pencil through the wire to create a tiny hole. Thread the end of the curtain tassel through the hole and tie it in a knot on the inside of the sieve to secure it in place. Once the glue has thoroughly dried, your cheese safe is ready to use.

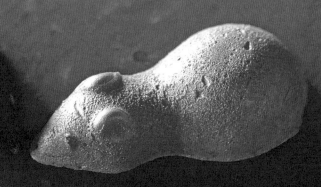

Sugared almonds were originally invented by a French apothecary. He had the idea of encasing almonds in sugar and honey to preserve them and make them easier to transport. It was thought that almonds freshened the breath and were good for digestion and fighting infertility. This is why they came to be found regularly on French tables at major events, such as weddings and christenings. The tradition remains popular – at the countless weddings I have been to, there has almost always been a little bag of sugared almonds at my table. To add a personal touch, you can't beat making your own and presenting them in a homemade tin (see pages 30–1). Experiment with a variety of nuts, as many are just as tasty prepared in this way.

PREP TIME:
10 minutes

TOTAL TIME:
1 hour, plus 24 hours for setting

MAKES:
1kg (2lb 4oz)

SUGARED NUTS

1kg (2lb 4oz) whole nuts (use blanched almonds, macadamia nuts or a mixture)

3 free-range egg whites

450g (1lb) icing sugar

5 drops of food colouring (optional – traditionally, sugared almonds come in pastel pink, yellow, blue and green)

1 Preheat the oven to 180ºC/fan 160ºC/gas mark 4. Line a couple of large baking sheets with nonstick baking paper.

2 Spread out the nuts in a single layer on the baking sheets, then toast in the oven for 5–10 minutes until they are light golden in colour. Remove from the oven and leave to cool.

3 Line 2 clean, cool baking sheets with silicone mats or nonstick baking paper.

4 In a food mixer, beat together the egg whites and icing sugar until thick. Add the food colouring, if liked.

5 Dip each nut, one at a time, into the sugar mixture, then remove it with a fork and allow any excess sugar mixture to drip off. Transfer the coated nuts to the lined baking sheets and allow to set (this can take a while – be prepared to let them sit for at least 24 hours).

⌐How to⌐ Make
Decorated Tins

It's the little touches like this that will add the 'wow' factor to your event. Simply follow the basic steps below to add the illustrations opposite to your tins and your guests will have a keepsake they can remember your day by for ever.

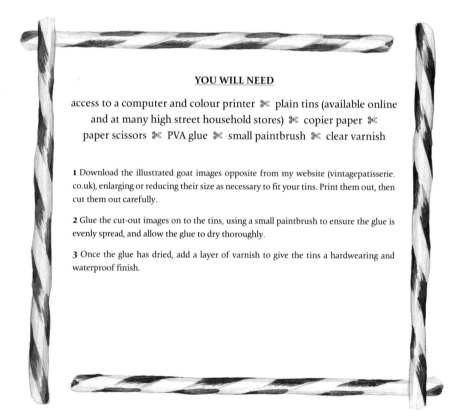

YOU WILL NEED

access to a computer and colour printer ✄ plain tins (available online and at many high street household stores) ✄ copier paper ✄ paper scissors ✄ PVA glue ✄ small paintbrush ✄ clear varnish

1 Download the illustrated goat images opposite from my website (vintagepatisserie. co.uk), enlarging or reducing their size as necessary to fit your tins. Print them out, then cut them out carefully.

2 Glue the cut-out images on to the tins, using a small paintbrush to ensure the glue is evenly spread, and allow the glue to dry thoroughly.

3 Once the glue has dried, add a layer of varnish to give the tins a hardwearing and waterproof finish.

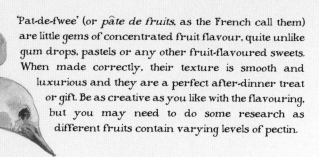

'Pat-de-fwee' (or *pâte de fruits*, as the French call them) are little gems of concentrated fruit flavour, quite unlike gum drops, pastels or any other fruit-flavoured sweets. When made correctly, their texture is smooth and luxurious and they are a perfect after-dinner treat or gift. Be as creative as you like with the flavouring, but you may need to do some research as different fruits contain varying levels of pectin.

Fruit Jellies

PREP TIME:
15 minutes

TOTAL TIME:
15 minutes, plus 12 hours for setting

MAKES:
18 squares

nonstick baking spray, for greasing (optional)

300ml (½ pint) fruit juice (use any flavour, but apple is great)

25g (1oz) powdered gelatine

500g (1lb 2oz) granulated sugar

500g (1lb 2oz) fruit jam

1 Line a 20cm (8in) square roasting tin with some nonstick baking paper. Alternatively, use a silicone fruit jelly mould in the shape and size of your choice, sprayed with nonstick baking spray.

2 Pour half the fruit juice into a small bowl or measuring cup and sprinkle over the gelatine. Leave to sit for 5 minutes.

3 In a saucepan, combine the remaining juice with 300g (10½oz) of the sugar. Bring to the boil over a medium-high heat and cook, stirring, for about 5 minutes until the sugar dissolves.

4 Add the jam and whisk to combine. Return the mixture to the boil and cook for about 2 minutes until it is thick and syrupy. Turn off the heat, add the gelatine mixture and whisk until the gelatine dissolves. Pour the mixture through a fine sieve into the prepared tin. Refrigerate until set, which will take at least 12 hours.

5 Place the remaining sugar in a pie plate or shallow bowl. Cut the fruit jelly into 2.5cm (1in) squares and toss in the sugar to coat just before serving.

◦ HOW TO MAKE
SAUCY CUBES

The appeal of the Flying Saucer is undeniable – who can resist the array of colours and the explosions of tangy sherbet? These sugary disc-shaped capsules were originally used to give doses of powdered medicine a more pleasant taste. Inspired by this idea, Astra Sweets launched Flying Saucers in sweet form in the late 1960s. Their timing was impeccable – the world was enraptured with all things space age, NASA's expedition to the moon was in the media and the film *2001: A Space Odyssey* had just become a box office hit. My Saucy Cubes are a cubic take on the famous disc-shaped sweets, but with more sherbet and more rice paper.

YOU WILL NEED

ruler ✄ piece of card ✄ A4 sheet of rice paper ✄ pin ✄ paper scissors ✄ fine paintbrush
✄ edible glue (*see* box, below) ✄ homemade sherbet (*see* page 128)

1 Measure a 2cm (¾in) square on the card, then cut it out.

2 Place the card square on the reverse side of the rice paper. Use the pin head to score around it six times to create the configuration of squares shown in the shape below, then add tabs, using a ruler to help you achieve straight lines.

3 Now cut out the shape. Bend the rice paper at the score marks to assemble the cube. Using a fine paintbrush, apply edible glue to one tab, position the glued tab in place on the inner surface of the cube and hold for a few seconds to secure. Repeat with all but one of the tabs to secure your shape.

4 Pour in your homemade sherbet and secure the remaining tab with edible glue.

EDIBLE GLUE

I use this fantastic invention to hold the rice paper sides together when making Saucy Cubes. Put ¼ tsp tylose powder (*see* page 154) into a small bowl and add 2 tbsp warm water. Stir with a fork to break up the lumps of powder as best you can (the mixture will look lumpy – this is normal). Cover the bowl and leave the mixture in the refrigerator overnight. When it has set, it will have a syrupy consistency. If it's too thick, add more water. If it's too thin, add more tylose powder. Use a paintbrush to apply the glue with precision.

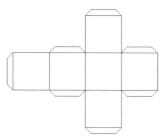

Parma Violets are a firm favourite of mine – perhaps it's because my granny always smelled of violets! Similar to Love Hearts (*see pages 44–5*) these classic British sweets are traditionally made using an 8-ton press, but this homemade version requires no heavy kit. The beauty in making them is that you can inscribe them! (*For guidance on how to do this, see page 17.*)

PARMA VIOLETS

PREP TIME:
10 minutes

TOTAL TIME:
1 hour, plus 24 hours for drying

MAKES: 80–100

1 tsp glucose syrup

4 tbsp hot water

7g (1/₀₀oz) powdered gelatine

450g (1lb) icing sugar, plus extra for dusting

5 drops of violet food colouring

½ tsp violet flavouring

1 Place the syrup and water into the bowl of a food mixer and whisk to combine. Then stir in the gelatine until it is well distributed.

2 Swap your mixer's whisk attachment for the paddle attachment. Add roughly one-quarter of the icing sugar and mix slowly until it is incorporated. Then add another quarter, again mixing on a low setting until the mixture comes together like a dough. Pause between additions to allow the sugar to mix in thoroughly. Continue in this way until all the icing sugar has been added. Every once in a while, stop the mixer and scrape down the bottom and sides of the bowl. The mixture will change from a thin, watery liquid to a very stiff dough.

3 Once all of the sugar has been added, dust a work surface with icing sugar and scrape out the mixture on to the work surface. Generously dust the top of the mixture with more icing sugar, then begin to knead it as if it were bread dough, folding the ball of dough over on to itself, then using the heel of your hand to push it down. Give the dough a quarter-turn and repeat the process, dusting it with more icing sugar as often as necessary to prevent it from sticking to the board or your hands. Knead until the mixture is satiny and not sticky, then press it into a disc shape.

4 Add the violet food colouring and flavouring to the centre of the disc and fold it over on itself. (It is a good idea to wear disposable plastic gloves during this step to keep your hands free of colours and odours.) Knead the dough ball just as you did before until the colour is evenly dispersed throughout and all streaks have disappeared.

5 Cover the dough in clingfilm to stop it drying out while you roll and press your sweets. Cut off a piece of dough and roll it into a thick sausage shape, then cut this down into individual sweet-sized portions. Roll each of these into a ball, then use your hand to press it into a flat round that has a diameter of roughly 1–2cm (½–¾in). Alternatively, you could improvise a shaping and cutting tool that will result in your desired shape. For instance, if you have a bottle with a tiny lid, you can use the lid to shape and press the sweets into uniform rounds. Dust the item you use to shape the sweets with icing sugar so it doesn't stick to the dough. Leave the pressed sweets on a sheet of nonstick baking paper as you work on the remaining dough. Continue until you have used up all the dough.

6 Allow your sweets to air-dry for 24 hours, then store them in an airtight container at room temperature.

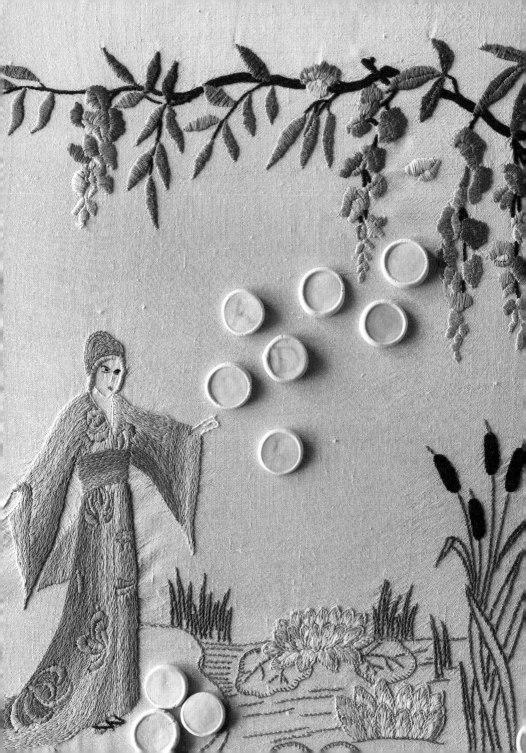

If, like me, you are a fan of violets, you will love this cocktail. Elegant in style and floral in flavour, it's a vintage delight. And if you're in the mood to show off, a decoration of delicate edible flowers is just the ticket.

PARMA VIOLET COCKTAIL

PREP TIME:
10 minutes

TOTAL TIME:
15 minutes

MAKES: 4

FOR THE VIOLET SYRUP

100ml (3½fl oz) water

100g (3½oz) granulated sugar

¼ tsp violet flavouring

5 drops of violet colouring

FOR THE COCKTAIL

50ml (2fl oz) peach schnapps

50ml (2fl oz) violet syrup
(*see* left)

1 tbsp lime juice

200ml (⅓ pint) sparkling water

50ml (2fl oz) vodka

crushed ice

violet flowers, to decorate (optional)

1 To make the violet syrup, combine the water and sugar in a saucepan and place the pan over a high heat. Bring to the boil, then reduce the heat and simmer for 5 minutes.

2 Take the pan off the heat and add the flavouring and colouring. Leave in the refrigerator to cool for 30 minutes.

3 When you're ready to make the cocktail, combine all the ingredients in a cocktail shaker. Strain into chilled glasses, decorated with violet flowers, if using, and serve immediately.

Creamy and crunchy, the Jazzie is unrivalled. My brother and I would always choose them on our weekly visit to the sweet shop on pocket money day. Later we would sit in front of the TV and work our way through our small white paper bags full of sugary delights, trying to count the Hundreds and Thousands on top of the Jazzies. As there are only two elements to this recipe, you can play around and have some fun. Jazzies make great gifts and, due to chef's privilege, you get to lick the bowl!

PREP TIME:
10 minutes

TOTAL TIME:
20 minutes,
plus 10 minutes
for freezing

MAKES: 16

Jazzies

200g (7oz) chocolate (milk, dark or white,
or a combination)
40g (1½oz) Hundreds and Thousands
(try multi-coloured, red, white and blue)

1 You'll need a baking sheet that has a lip around the edges or a meringue tin that measures roughly 28 × 18cm (11 × 7in). Line it with nonstick baking paper.

2 Break the chocolate into pieces and melt it in a bowl set over a saucepan of barely simmering water, making sure that the base of the bowl doesn't touch the water.

3 Pour the chocolate on to the lined baking sheet and use a spatula to spread it out in a thin, even layer. (Alternatively, you could pour the chocolate into a jug that is easy to pour from and then pour chocolate shapes directly on to the lined baking paper.) Sprinkle the Hundreds and Thousands over the chocolate in an even layer. Place the baking sheet in the freezer to enable the chocolate to set.

4 After 5 minutes in the freezer, take out the baking sheet and score the chocolate into 16 rectangles. Return it to the freezer for about another 5 minutes to finish setting. Once the chocolate sheet has set, use the score marks on the surface to help you break it into smaller rectangular pieces.

This cocktail is dedicated to the 'sweet tooth tribe'! If you are looking for fun rather than sophistication, this is your golden ticket!

Jazzies Cocktail

PREP TIME:
5 minutes

TOTAL TIME:
10 minutes,
plus 15 minutes
for drying

MAKES: 2

1 free-range egg white, beaten for 1 minute, until frothy

50g (1¾oz) Hundreds and Thousands

150ml (¼ pint) milk

50ml (2fl oz) chocolate liqueur

50ml (2fl oz) chocolate syrup

1 Put the egg white on a small saucer. Dip the rims of your cocktail glasses into it, then dip them into a plate spread with the Hundreds and Thousands to form colourful rims. Leave to dry for 15 minutes.

2 In a cocktail shaker, mix the milk, liqueur and syrup, shaking well. Pour carefully into the prepared glasses and serve immediately.

There are 134 different messages to be found on the iconic Love Heart sweet, though some have been abandoned, such as 'Hey Daddio' and 'Far Out, Man', while modern replacements – such as 'Email Me' – have been added. As a child I remember passing around sweets with messages of affection, nervously giggling and running away as the recipient read it! Like Parma Violets, Love Hearts are traditionally formed from a powdered mixture being pressed by 8 tons of pressure. However, this homemade version can be done without heavy machinery! I love the idea of inscribing an initial or two on the sweets, which makes for perfect wedding favours. (For guidance on how to do this, *see* page 17.)

Love Hearts

PREP TIME:
5 minutes

TOTAL TIME:
1 hour, plus 24 hours
for drying

MAKES: about 100

125ml (4fl oz) water

7g (¹⁄₀oz) powdered gelatine

2 tsp glucose syrup

900g (2lb) icing sugar, plus extra for dusting

15g (½oz) citric acid, finely crushed

10 drops of food colouring (pale colours work best –
try pink, yellow, green or blue)

1 tsp flavouring (try vanilla, almond, lemon, orange or mint)

edible markers in the colours of your choice

1 Place half of the water in a small bowl and sprinkle over the gelatine. Leave to stand for 5 minutes.

2 Place the remaining water in a small saucepan over a low heat and stir in the glucose syrup. Once the water is hot, add the gelatine mixture and stir until it has all dissolved.

3 Pour the mixture into the bowl of a food mixer fitted with a paddle attachment. Add a quarter of the icing sugar and mix slowly until it is incorporated. Then add another quarter, again mixing on a low setting. Pause between additions to allow the sugar to mix in. Continue in this way until all the icing sugar has been incorporated. Every once in a while,

stop the mixer and scrape down the bottom and sides of the bowl. The mixture will change from a thin, watery liquid to a very stiff dough.

4 Dust a work surface with icing sugar and scrape the mixture out on to the surface. It will be very sticky and stiff. Generously dust the top of the mixture and begin to knead it as if it were bread dough, folding the ball of dough over on to itself, then using the heel of your hand to push it down. Give the mixture a quarter-turn and repeat the process, dusting it with more icing sugar as often as necessary to prevent it from sticking to the work surface or your hands. Knead until the mixture is satiny and not sticky.

5 Add the citric acid to the mixture and knead for a few minutes more until it has been evenly distributed.

6 Decide how many colours and flavours you wish to add and divide the mixture into the number of portions you need – 5 portions works well with this quantity of mixture. Wrap each portion in clingfilm until you are ready to flavour and colour it. Take 1 portion and flatten it into a palm-sized disc. Add 2 drops of food colouring and $^1/_5$ tsp flavouring to the centre of the disc and fold it over on itself. (It is a good idea to wear disposable plastic gloves during this step to keep your hands free of colours and odours.) Knead the mixture as you did before until the colour is evenly dispersed throughout and all streaks have disappeared. Repeat this process with the remaining portions, using different colours and flavours for each.

7 You can shape the sweets either by pressing them by hand or by cutting them using icing cutters in your chosen shape – perhaps heart-shaped ones! If pressing, roll each portion of the mixture into a sausage shape and use a knife to cut it into individual discs. Press each disc between finger and thumb to flatten it, then set it aside to dry on a sheet of nonstick baking paper. If using icing cutters, dust your work surface and a rolling pin with icing sugar and roll out 1 of the coloured and flavoured portions to your desired thickness. Use an icing cutter to cut out individual sweets. Repeat with the remaining balls of mixture. Now leave your sweets to dry for 24 hours before serving them or storing in an airtight container at room temperature.

Fudge Hearts

If you are feeling in the mood for love but don't have the time to make my Love Hearts (*see* pages 44–5), here is a delicious alternative. Fudge Hearts are very simple to make and are perfect for chocolate lovers. I'm quite sure you could steal a heart or two by making these! (For guidance on how to emboss your sweets with personal messages, *see* page 17.)

FUDGE HEARTS

PREP TIME:
5 minutes

TOTAL TIME:
40 minutes,
plus 50 minutes for
cooling and freezing

MAKES: 24

700g (1lb 9oz) finely chopped white chocolate
(or use white chocolate chips)

397g can sweetened condensed milk

20 drops of food colouring (use 4 drops per colour
– try pink, yellow, green, lavender and white)

nonstick baking spray, for greasing

1 To make the fudge, heat the white chocolate and condensed milk in a bowl set over a saucepan of barely simmering water, ensuring the base of the bowl doesn't touch the water. Stir frequently until about half of the chocolate is melted. Take the pan off the heat and leave the mixture to sit for 2 minutes, then stir until all the chocolate is melted and the mixture is smooth. (If you overheat this creamy white fudge, it will become greasy as the cocoa butter may seep out of the chocolate. If that happens, the best way to salvage the fudge is to cool it down by spreading it on marble or granite and kneading it until the cocoa butter mixes back into the fudge.)

2 Divide the fudge into 5 equal portions and place each portion in a bowl. Stir a different colour of food colouring into each, adding a drop at a time until you achieve the colours you want. Allow the fudge to cool and thicken for 30 minutes.

3 Scoop some fudge out of a bowl and knead it with your hands until it is smooth. Pinch off about a tablespoonful and roll it into a ball. Set this in one of the heart-shaped cavities of a silicone heart-shaped mould that has been sprayed with nonstick baking spray. Press the mixture into the cavity to flatten it. Remove any mixture that doesn't fit into the cavity. Really press down on the fudge, eliminating any air bubbles or holes. Continue in this way until all the mixture is used. (If the fudge is greasy and a bit separated, just knead small portions of the mixture between the palms of your hands before placing it into the moulds. This will help to smooth out the mix before it sets in the moulds. Wipe the excess grease off your hands before rolling the next heart.)

4 Place the filled mould in the freezer for 20 minutes. Remove the hearts from the moulds to serve, or store them in an airtight container at room temperature.

I remember making Easter eggs at school as if it were yesterday. Every year, our teachers invented new and wondrous creations for us to make using the humble egg. On Easter Sunday I would present my Dad with his 'egg' and was so excited for him to open it up to see it was not a real egg but full of sweet yumminess. This is a fun edible Easter gift to make with all the family.

Easter 'Eggs'

6 free-range eggs, at room temperature

FOR THE GANACHE

150g (5½oz) dark chocolate, broken into small pieces

150ml (¼ pint) double cream

2 tsp liqueur or rum

FOR THE LIME JELLY

150ml (¼ pint) water

7g (¹⁄₆oz) powdered gelatine

100g (3½oz) granulated sugar

2 tbsp lime juice

3 drops of green food colouring

PREP TIME:
20 minutes

TOTAL TIME:
1 hour, plus 2 hours
for setting

MAKES: 6

1 To blow an egg's contents out of the shell, you need to make a hole at each end of the egg using an electric hobby drill, a little hand drill or a good-sized needle. The hole at the pointed end can be quite large, with a diameter of roughly 1cm (½in), as you will be filling the egg through this hole. Once you've made the holes, break the yolk by inserting a bamboo skewer and wiggling it about. Next blow into the smaller hole with an open mouth, lips sealed around the hole, to empty the contents into a bowl and discard them.

2 Rinse the empty eggshells in a bowl of water. Drain and rinse repeatedly until the water runs clear, then place the shells, with the holes facing down, in the egg carton for 20 minutes to allow them to dry. I dry the shells in the microwave to ensure that they are completely clean, heating them for 12-second bursts, 4–6 times. If you do the same, remember that these eggs are hot when you take them out of the microwave, so take care: it's easy to forget – trust me!

3 Now make the ganache. Put the chocolate into a heatproof bowl. Heat the cream in a small saucepan until it just comes to the boil, then pour it over the chocolate. Leave for 1 minute, then stir until the chocolate melts. Add the liqueur or rum at this stage.

4 Sit the egg shells in the egg carton with the holes facing up and, using a funnel, pour ganache into each egg until it is three-quarters full. Transfer the carton to the refergerator and leave it for 1 hour to allow the ganache to set.

5 Meanwhile make the lime jelly. Pour 50ml (2fl oz) of the water into a bowl and sprinkle over the gelatine.

6 Place the remaining water and the sugar in a saucepan. Bring to the boil and continue to boil for 1–2 minutes until the mixture has a syrupy consistency. Remove it from the heat and add the lime juice and food colouring. Stir in the gelatine mixture until it is completely dissolved.

7 Using a funnel, pour the lime jelly on top of the set ganache until the egg shells are full. Leave the eggs to set in the refrigerator for 1 hour. Crack half of the egg shell off the top before serving.

Scratch Cards for an Easter Egg Hunt

Easter 'Eggs'

How to Make
Scratch Cards for
an Easter Egg Hunt

I'm an Aries baby, so my birthday always falls in the Easter holidays. When I was young, my parents would make an extra fuss of this holiday to ensure I was feeling utterly special, and part of this was to organise an Easter egg hunt every year. We would sometimes be finding eggs months later, which just enhanced the thrill! This simple hunt will keep children occupied for hours.

YOU WILL NEED

Easter eggs, shop bought or homemade (*see* page 49) ✄ access to a computer and printer ✄ some A4 sheets of coloured card (ensure they are thin enough to go through your printer) ✄ sticky back plastic ✄ paper scissors ✄ silver acrylic paint ✄ washing-up liquid ✄ paintbrush

1 First of all, think of a place to hide your Easter eggs. Choose carefully, as you will need the same number of scratch cards as there are letters in the name of your hiding place. (So, for example, if your hiding place is a toy box, you will need 6 cards – T-O-Y-B-O-X.)

2 Download the scratch card frame illustration opposite from my website (vintagepatisserie.co.uk). Print the correct number of copies of the frame on to coloured card. (Alternatively, you can photocopy the page opposite on to coloured paper, then stick the paper on to some card for strength.)

3 Cut out the cards. Turn them all over and, on the blank sides, write one letter on each card, spelling out the name of the hiding place. (Don't forget to hide your Easter egg hunt prizes in the place you've spelled out!) Cover the side of the cards with the letters with sticky back plastic, applying the plastic from one end of the card to the other, gently smoothing out air bubbles as you go. Use the scissors to cut off any excess.

4 Mix two parts silver acrylic paint with one part washing-up liquid. Paint over the plastic to completely obscure the letters, and leave to dry.

5 Now it's time to come up with clues! Turn the cards over and write one clue on each card, inside the printed frames. Each clue needs to lead to the place where the following clue will be hidden. For example, the first clue – which you will hand to the children – might lead to a bookshelf, then the next clue could be hidden in the kitchen and so on. The children will find the cards and collect them as they work through the clues.

6 Hide the cards and let the hunt begin. Once the children have collected all the cards, they can frantically scratch off all the silver panels and rearrange the letters to spell out the hiding place for all the Easter booty!

SOFTBALL, FIRMBALL & HARDBALL SWEETS

By this time, you know that a humble bag of sugar can be transformed into the stuff of dreams. Now that you and sugar are intimate, it's time to make your relationship even more meaningful! In this chapter, I show you what happens to sugar when it is heated to temperatures above 112°C (234°F). This level of heat allows you to manipulate it however you wish, so cut loose your creativity and see what flights of fancy you come up with as you make my recipes yours. Of course, there are more old favourites to be found here – Marshmallows, Fudge, Toffee Bonbons, Liquorice, Gumdrops, Fondants (or Fun-dents, as I like to call mine), Wine Gums and Edinburgh Rock, for instance. And the recipe for Turkish Delight (my Mum's favourite) even comes with instructions for making a fantastic Secret Hollow Book in which to hide it (because it's just too good to share!) or give it as a gift (if you really must).

If you ever attend a party of mine, you'll realise that I'm a fan of rose. I may offer you rose tea, rose cocktail or even rose sandwiches! So it's no surprise that Turkish delight – with its sweet rose-flavoured jelly – holds a special place in my childhood memories. But it wasn't until I was around 10 years old that I tasted the traditional (real) deal, which came in a variety of flavours – nut, date, orange and, of course, rose! I love this gooey orange and pistachio combination.

TURKISH DELIGHT

PREP TIME:
20 minutes
TOTAL TIME:
45 minutes, plus 3–4 hours for setting
MAKES:
20 squares

butter, for greasing

icing sugar, for dusting

350ml (12fl oz) water

600g (1lb 5oz) caster sugar

3 tbsp golden syrup

125ml (4fl oz) orange juice

3 tbsp grated orange rind (about 4 large oranges)

20g (¾oz) powdered gelatine

100g (3½oz) cornflour

125ml (4fl oz) cold water

flavouring (1 tbsp vanilla extract, 1½ tsp rose water or ½ tsp mint extract)

5–8 drops of red food colouring

100g (3½oz) pistachio nuts, chopped (optional)

1 Grease a 20cm (8in) square cake tin and line it with nonstick silicone baking paper. Give the lining a generous sprinkling of sifted icing sugar.

2 Put the water, caster sugar and golden syrup in a large saucepan and bring to the boil over a medium-high heat. When the mixture comes to the boil, remove the sugar crystals that are stuck to the inside of the pan above the bubbling solution (*see page 17*). Continue to boil the mixture, without stirring, until it reaches 116°C (240°F) – the softball stage.

3 Meanwhile, stir together the orange juice and rind in a jug or small bowl, sprinkle over the gelatine, stir again, then set aside.

4 In a small bowl, dissolve the cornflour in the cold water. When the sugar mixture has reached the softball stage, stir in the cornflour mix. Put the pan over a medium-low heat and simmer, stirring gently, until the mixture is very thick – this will take only a couple of minutes.

5 Remove the pan from the heat and stir in the orange juice mixture, the flavouring of your choice, the food colouring and the pistachios, if liked. Pour the Turkish Delight mixture into the prepared tin and leave to set in a cool, dry place (not in the refrigerator), which should take 3–4 hours. When cool, sprinkle the top with a thick layer of sifted icing sugar. Cut into 20 cubes and roll them in sifted icing sugar. Knock off any excess sugar, then pack away in an airtight container and store at room temperature. Alternatively, hide it away in a homemade Secret Hollow Book (*see page 60*).

How to Make a
Secret Hollow book

When my granny bought me my first box of Turkish delight, I remember being wooed by the jewel-like box that it came in. The presentation of gifts is everything! By taking the time to track down a beautiful old book (which cost pennies in second-hand shops) you can turn it into a Secret Hollow Book and create a gift that someone special can treasure forever.

YOU WILL NEED

beautiful hardback vintage book (you can pick one up cheaply in junk shops, charity shops or at car boot sales) ✄ newspaper ✄ PVA glue and container to mix it in ✄ small paintbrush ✄ £1 coin (to use as a spacer) ✄ metal ruler ✄ pencil ✄ sharp scalpel or craft knife ✄ clear varnish (optional)

1 Lay out a few sheets of newspaper to protect your work surface, then mix up a glue solution of PVA and water in a 50:50 ratio.

2 Flick past the book's title pages to the first page of full text – this will be your first cut-out page. Turn this page over, too. You will cut this page last (this will make sense later on!). Hold the bulk of the book together and brush the outside edges with the glue solution. Use enough to stick them together – you may need two coats.

3 Put the £1 coin into the book on top of the first glued page and below the unglued pages. Close the book and allow it to dry. Once it is dry, remove the coin and stick the back cover to the glued pages and allow to dry again.

4 Open your book to the first glued page and, using a metal ruler, draw a rectangular border 2.5cm (1in) from the edges of the page. Carefully and slowly cut along the lines using the scalpel or craft knife, resting the blade against the metal ruler as you cut. Keep the blade vertical or the hole will slope as you cut deeper into the book. Continue cutting until you are on the last page.

5 Remove the cut-out paper, then brush the inside of the cut-out hollow with PVA solution, then brush glue on the top of the first glued page. Now turn over the first loose page on to the glue, this will stick it to the glued and cut-out section of the book. Close the book and leave to dry thoroughly.

6 Open the book to the first page before the cut-out section, which is now glued to the cut-out section. Carefully cut out the shape of the rectangle of the hollow beneath this page using the scalpel or craft knife, covering your earlier pencil markings and creating a neat finish on your top page. As an optional extra, you can now brush the entire inside of the hollow with a coat of clear varnish, so that you can wipe it clean after storing sweeties inside! And then you're done and ready to fill your hollow book with secret sweet treats.

There are some flavour combinations that you need to test to validate the hype. Rose and cucumber is one of them. I'm not sure why this cocktail is so delicious. I can only presume that it's down to the combined sweetness of the rose, the sharpness of the gin and the freshness of the cucumber.

ENGLISH DELIGHT

6 fine slices of cucumber

45ml (1½fl oz) Hendrick's Gin

30ml (1fl oz) crème de rose or rose syrup

ice cubes

125ml (4fl oz) lemonade

PREP TIME:
10 minutes

TOTAL TIME:
10 minutes

MAKES: 2

1 For the cucumber 'flower' garnish, place 2 slices of cucumber flat on top of one another, with the smallest of them on the top. Fold the third slice in half, then in quarters, so it resembles a flower and has a triangle shape. Place the first 2 slices in the bottom of a glass then place the folded one on top. Repeat for the second glass.

2 Mix the gin, crème de rose or rose syrup and ice in a cocktail shaker.

3 Pour the cocktail into your 2 glasses, over the top of the garnish, top up with lemonade and serve immediately.

I'd never tasted homemade marshmallows until my later years. They were so light that they disappeared in a puff quite unlike the ones I had as a child! Making them from scratch allows you to flavour them with anything you want – in that way you can transform the humble marshmallow into something quite indulgent and suitable for grown-ups.

Marshmallows

PREP TIME:
20 minutes

TOTAL TIME:
50 minutes, plus 4 hours for setting

MAKES:
20 squares

butter or nonstick spray, for greasing
300–400g (10½–14oz) icing sugar
225ml (8fl oz) cold water
20g (¾oz) powdered gelatine
400g (14oz) granulated sugar
240ml (9fl oz) golden syrup
¼ tsp salt
2 tsp mint extract (or use 2 tsp vanilla extract, ½ tsp almond extract or 2 tsp lemon or orange extract)

1 Lightly grease the base of a 33 × 23 × 5cm (13 × 9 × 2in) baking sheet. Line the base of the sheet with nonstick silicone baking paper, then sift about 3 tbsp of the icing sugar on to the base.

2 Put half the cold water into the bowl of a food mixer and sprinkle over the gelatine. Don't switch on the motor just yet!

3 Put the granulated sugar, golden syrup, salt and the remaining cold water into a saucepan. Stir over a medium heat until the sugar dissolves and the mixture comes to the boil. When it does, remove the sugar crystals that are stuck to the inside of the pan above the bubbling solution (*see page 17*). Increase the heat and boil, without stirring, until the syrup reaches 116°C (240°F) – the softball stage. Remove from the heat.

4 Run your food processor on a low setting as you slowly pour the hot syrup into the gelatine mixture in a thin stream down the side of the bowl. Once it's all in, gradually increase the speed to high and beat for at least 10 minutes. The mixture will triple in volume. Add the flavouring and beat for another minute.

5 Scrape or pour the marshmallow mixture on to the prepared baking sheet and spread it with a damp spatula. Then sift 3–4 tbsp icing sugar over the mallow and leave to stand, uncovered, at room temperature for about 4 hours until set.

6 Remove the marshmallow from the baking sheet by running a small sharp knife around the edge to loosen it. Turn it out on to a surface dusted with lots more sifted icing sugar. Peel off the silicone paper and cover the top with plenty more sifted icing sugar.

7 Cut the marshmallow into 20 squares using kitchen scissors, a pizza roller or a sharp knife. Dip the cut sides of the sweets in additional icing sugar. Shake off any excess sugar and store the marshmallows in an airtight container at room temperature.

MiNT RoYal HoT MocHa

250ml (9fl oz) warm milk

45ml (1½fl oz) hot coffee

25g (1oz) grated milk or dark chocolate

45ml (1½fl oz) Royal Chocolate Mint Liqueur

1 marshmallow (see page 62)

It would be a travesty not to dip your marshmallows into something delicious, sweet and hot. This cocktail is a special treat. Just think of it as in incredible after-dinner mint!

PREP TIME: 10 minutes

TOTAL TIME: 15 minutes

MAKES: 1

1 Add the warm milk to the shot of coffee in a big mug. Stir in the grated chocolate and continue to stir until it has melted.

2 Add the chocolate mint liqueur and marshmallow to the hot drink and serve immediately.

How to Make
Animal Candle Holders

Whatever your age, toasting marshmallows is always fun. As you get older, you can appreciate the caramelized sweetness straight from the flame. And, with this quirky set of candleholders, you don't have to wait until Guy Fawkes night to get cooking! The method below can be adapted to any four-legged animals. No animals were hurt during the making of this craft project.

YOU WILL NEED

drill ✄ a selection of four-legged plastic toy animals ✄ clamp ✄ pen ✄ newspaper ✄ flame-retardant white spray paint ✄ small tapered candles

1 Select a drill bit that is of a similar size to your candles and attach it to your drill.

2 Secure one of the plastic animals in a clamp so you can safely drill a hole into its back. Using a pen, mark the spot at which you would like to drill.

3 With the drill, carefully make a hole where marked. Use a gentle pressure while drilling as you want to ensure you don't drill all the way through the toy. Make the hole about 1cm (½in) deep.

4 Remove any loose bits of plastic created by the drilling. Then, in a well-ventilated area, lay out some sheets of newspaper to protect your work surface and spray the entire toy with the spray paint. You may need several coats to achieve an even coverage.

5 Repeat the process with the other toy animals. Now simply add candles and your animal candle holders are ready to use.

It's fair to presume that your granny loved fondants and I bet many of you would have made them with her as a child. I did – we coloured ours with pastel shades and scented them with rose or lavender. Here, I have given them an update, making them black and white in colour and flavouring them with zesty lemon and refreshing mint.

FUN-DENTS

PREP TIME:
10 minutes

TOTAL TIME:
1 hour, plus 30 minutes
for setting

MAKES:
about 20

450g (1lb) granulated sugar

350ml (12fl oz) water

¼ tsp cream of tartar

¼ tsp lemon juice

½ tsp flavouring (use peppermint, lemon, almond or vanilla)

5 drops each of red, black, beige or yellow food colouring

1 Put the sugar, water, cream of tartar and lemon juice in a large heavy-based saucepan and heat, stirring, over a medium heat until the sugar is dissolved. Now cover the pan with a lid and boil for 3 minutes.

2 Uncover the pan and insert a sugar thermometer that has been heated under a hot tap and cook, without stirring, until the mixture reaches 116°C (240°F) – the softball stage. Remove from the heat and, when the fondant has cooled to 43°C (110°F), scrape the mixture in from the edges using a spatula, working in towards the centre repeatedly for about 15 minutes until the mixture thickens and whitens.

3 Now add the flavourings and colourings. If you're making 2 colours of sweets, halve the mixture after adding the flavouring, then add a colour to each half. Now continue to knead until the mixture is velvety. Wrap the fondant in a cloth wrung out in cold water and set aside to 'season' for 30 minutes before use.

4 To shape the sweets to look like draught pieces, roll the fondant flat and use a shot glass or cutter the size of a draught piece to cut the pieces. Lastly, imprint the design of a clean draughts piece in the fondant.

BEAT THEM & EAT THEM
AN AFTER-DINNER GAME

The rules of this game are very similar to the game of draughts, with one important difference – when you capture your opponent's pieces you get to eat or drink them! Instead of ordinary draughts pieces, the game is played using Fun-dents and liqueur shots. The rules are as follows:

- Take 12 'pieces' of one colour and place one on each of the black squares in the first 3 rows of your side. Your opponent does the same with the other colour.

- Pieces are moved diagonally, one square at a time, on the black squares, towards the opponent's side of the board. The object of the game is to capture all of your opponent's pieces by hopping over them diagonally, landing in a vacant space. Once captured, you must eat or drink the piece, depending on whether it is a Fun-dent or a shot of liqueur.

- If a 'piece' reaches the other side of the board, it becomes a king. When this happens, place a spare Fun-dent on top to crown it. It can now move backwards, forwards and diagonally in any direction, moving one space per go.

- The winner is the first person to capture (and consume!) all of their opponent's pieces.

I remember the feelings I had on entering a fudge shop for the first time as if it were yesterday. It was like Fudge Narnia! I was at a theme park (where you lose your sense with money!) and I was overwhelmed by the array of choices and the quantities on offer. They sold every flavour of fudge imaginable and some that I'd never even heard of, and I had the freedom to choose whatever I liked. I asked for countless different types but, disappointingly, many of them tasted similar – except for rum & raisin. This flavour has remained a firm favourite of mine to this day.

PREP TIME:
10 minutes

TOTAL TIME:
40 minutes, plus 3 hours for setting

MAKES:
24 squares

RUM & Raisin Fudge

50ml (2fl oz) dark rum
100g (3½oz) raisins, roughly chopped
100g (3½oz) butter, plus extra for greasing
397g can sweetened condensed milk
125ml (4fl oz) milk
450g (1lb) demerara sugar

1 Put the dark rum in a bowl and add the chopped raisins. Set aside to soak.

2 Grease a 20cm (8in) square cake tin and line it with nonstick baking paper.

3 Combine the remaining ingredients in a large nonstick saucepan over a medium heat and stir until the sugar dissolves. Then remove the sugar crystals that are stuck to the inside of the pan above the bubbling solution (*see* page 17).

4 Bring the mixture to the boil, then simmer gently for 10–15 minutes, stirring constantly, until it reaches 116°C (240°F) – the softball stage.

5 Remove the saucepan from the heat and allow the temperature of the mixture to drop to 110°C (230°F) before beating it. Beat with a wooden spoon for 10 minutes until the mixture is very thick and almost has the consistency and look of smooth peanut butter. This step is vital for thickening the fudge, so ensure you beat the mixture until it is very thick and stiff.

6 Stir in the raisins and the rum, then pour the mixture into the prepared tin and set aside for about 3 hours to cool.

7 When the fudge is completely cold, cut it into 24 small squares using a sharp knife.

This boozy dessert really brings the wonderful combination of rum and raisin to life, and the addition of hot baked banana and cold velvety ice cream is a delightful treat.

ßaked ßaNaNas
WITH RUM & RaISIN ICe CReaM

PREP TIME: 15 minutes

TOTAL TIME: 40 minutes, plus 30 minutes cooling and 1 hour churning/freezing

MAKES: 500ml (18fl oz) ice cream and dessert for 4

FOR THE ICE CREAM

100ml (3½fl oz) milk

4 free-range egg yolks

60ml (2¼fl oz) golden syrup

1 tsp vanilla extract

1 tbsp black treacle

600ml (1 pint) double cream

100g (3½oz) Rum & Raisin Fudge (see page 68), chopped into small pieces

FOR THE BANANAS

20g (¾oz) unsalted butter

2 tbsp light brown sugar

2 bananas, peeled

2 tbsp dark rum

1 First, make the ice cream. Do this bit in advance as it needs time to freeze. Place the milk in a small saucepan over a medium heat and bring to just below boiling point, then remove from the heat.

2 While the milk is warming, put the egg yolks, golden syrup, vanilla extract and black treacle into the bowl of a freestanding food mixer and beat until thick and frothy (about 5 minutes). Now, slowly drizzle in the warm milk while the mixer is still on. Then transfer the mixture to a saucepan and heat very gently until it is thick enough to coat the back of a spoon.

3 Take the pan off the heat and add the cream. If you're using an ice-cream maker, cool the mixture in the refrigerator, then churn it according to the manufacturer's instructions. When the ice cream is nearly set and has the consistency of frozen yogurt, add the fudge. If you don't have an ice-cream maker, pour the mixture into a freezer-safe plastic container and freeze until it begins to harden. Then fold in the fudge pieces and freeze until the mixture is firm.

4 When you're ready to prepare the bananas for the dessert, put a saucepan on the stove over a medium heat. Place the butter and sugar in the pan and cook until it is dark and bubbling – this will take about 5 minutes. Meanwhile, slice the bananas.

5 Add the banana slices to the pan and cook for about 1 minute on each side until golden brown. Once cooked, add the rum. Cook for a further minute, then remove from the heat. Serve the warm banana and sauce with dollops of the ice cream.

During the 17th century, the English borrowed the word *bonbon* from France. Legend has it that a confectioner's apprentice called Tom Smith fell in love with the magical window displays he saw there, full as they were of enticing colour, and returned to these shores to create an inspired sweet. And so the bonbon was born! This recipe offers a softer version of this gorgeous toffee while honouring the soft colours of French-inspired confectionary. Feel free to make them any colour you wish!

TOFFEE BONBONS

PREP TIME:
10 minutes

TOTAL TIME:
50 minutes, plus
1–2 hours for setting

MAKES: 50

butter or nonstick baking spray, for greasing
300g (10½oz) light brown sugar
125ml (4fl oz) double cream
50g (1¾oz) butter, cut into small pieces
¼ tsp vanilla extract
1 tbsp liquid glucose
1 tbsp water
100g (3½oz) icing sugar, plus extra for dusting
15–20 drops of the food colouring of your choice (optional)

1 Grease a large baking sheet, preferably by spraying it with nonstick baking spray.

2 Put the sugar, cream, butter, vanilla extract, liquid glucose and water into a saucepan. Place the pan over a medium heat and stir constantly until the sugar is dissolved and the butter is melted. Continue to stir the mixture gently and slowly until it comes to the boil and, when it does, remove the sugar crystals that are stuck to the inside of the pan above the bubbling mixture (*see* page 17). Then boil the mixture, uncovered and without stirring, until it reaches 121°C (250°F) – the firmball stage. Do not stir while the mixture is boiling.

3 Pour 50 drops of the mixture, each about 2cm (¾in) wide, on to the prepared baking sheet. Allow to cool.

4 Sift the icing sugar into a bowl, add the food colouring and work it into the sugar thoroughly with a spatula. Then pass the whole lot through a fine sieve, working any lumps of the colouring through the mesh. Repeat this process a couple more times to ensure there are no more lumps and the icing sugar is evenly coloured.

5 Take each drop of caramel in turn and roll it into a sphere. Then toss it in the icing sugar and roll it around with a teaspoon. When each sweet is thoroughly coated, place it on a silicone mat, dust it lightly with more icing sugar and leave to set for 1–2 hours. Then knock off any excess sugar and serve the bonbons or store them in an airtight container.

How to Make
PAPER SPINNING TOPS

To celebrate the beauty and playful colours of the bonbon, I give you the spinning top! It's just as much fun for the kids to make these as to spin them and, I have to admit, they do look superb in a jar, ready for the next showdown!

YOU WILL NEED

metal ruler ✄ craft knife and cutting mat ✄ thin coloured paper in three or four colours (one sheet per colour will be adequate) ✄ glue or sticky tape ✄ cocktail sticks

1 Use a metal ruler and craft knife and cutting mat to cut the paper into long strips that are approximately 1cm (½in) wide and the length of an A4 sheet of paper.

2 Take a strip of paper and glue or tape one short end about 5mm (¼in) from one end of a cocktail stick. Then proceed to wrap the paper tightly around the stick, coiling it as neatly as possible to keep the paper aligned.

3 When you reach the end of the paper strip, take a different-coloured paper strip and glue or tape it to the end of the first strip, then continue rolling up tightly. Continue in this way until you have used four or five paper strips of varying colours. Now secure the end of the final strip with glue. You should have a disc that's about 2.5cm (1in) in diameter attached to the end of the cocktail stick. Allow the glue to dry.

4 Press the paper coil between your thumb and forefingers to shape the spinning top and create the silhouette you like.

I was never a fan of liquorice as a child. This stuck with me for years until I tried a toffee liquorice that was subtly scented with anise and had the smooth, creamy texture and mellow flavour of caramel. Gone was the 'break your teeth, dye your tongue black' liquorice square I remember! The version below encourages you to play around with cutting shapes and stamping letters for that personal touch. And you can double the amount of anise extract for a stronger liquorice flavour, if that's what you like.

PREP TIME:
30 minutes

TOTAL TIME:
45 minutes, plus at least
3 hours for setting

MAKES:
90 squares

liquorice

nonstick baking spray, for greasing

200g (7oz) butter

397g can sweetened condensed milk

450g (1lb) granulated sugar

250ml (9fl oz) corn syrup

pinch of salt

1 tsp anise extract (or use clove extract)

½ tsp black food colouring paste
(this can be found in craft and cake decorating
stores – *see* Resources, page 154)

1 Line a 23cm (9in) square cake tin with kitchen foil and spray with nonstick baking spray.

2 In quite a large saucepan, melt the butter over a medium heat. Once melted, add the condensed milk, sugar, corn syrup and salt and stir until combined.

3 Bring the mixture to the boil, stirring constantly. The mixture will darken as it heats up and you'll see some dark brown bits in it, but these won't affect the final product. Once it comes to the boil, continue to stir constantly to prevent it burning on the base of the pan. Attach a sugar thermometer and boil the mixture until it reaches 121ºC (250ºF) – the firmball stage.

4 Remove the mixture from the heat and stir in the anise extract and food colouring, mixing until thoroughly combined.

5 Pour the liquorice into the prepared cake tin. Allow it to set at room temperature – this could take anywhere from about 3 hours to overnight. Pop it into the refrigerator to speed up the process.

6 Cut the liquorice into 90 2.5cm (1in) squares using kitchen scissors. Alternatively, cut out different shapes and emboss them with a stamp so that they resemble Pontefract Cakes. Wrap individual sweets in waxed paper or clingfilm to store.

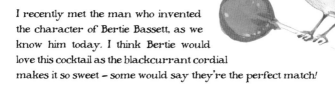

I recently met the man who invented
the character of Bertie Bassett, as we
know him today. I think Bertie would
love this cocktail as the blackcurrant cordial
makes it so sweet – some would say they're the perfect match!

Bertie's Blackcurrant

PREP TIME:
5 minutes

TOTAL TIME:
5 minutes

MAKES: 2

45ml (1½fl oz) Pastis
45ml (1½fl oz) blackcurrant cordial
45ml (1½fl oz) vodka
ice cubes
250ml (9fl oz) lemonade

1 Mix the Pastis, blackcurrant cordial
and vodka together in a cocktail
shaker. Pour the mixture into 2
cocktail glasses over ice and top up
with lemonade. Serve immediately.

Gumdrops won a place in my sweetie book due to their versatility. Sweet, chewy and full of flavour, they can be shaped in any mould. When I was very young, my Mum would always allow us to put one in the centre of her freshly baked fairy cakes!

GUMDROPS

PREP TIME:
5 minutes

TOTAL TIME:
25 minutes,
plus 1 hour for setting

MAKES: 25

400ml (14fl oz) cold water

20g (¾oz) powdered gelatine

300g (10½oz) granulated sugar

¼ tsp citric acid

½ tsp flavouring (try lime, lemon, almond or cinnamon)

3–5 drops of food colouring (try green, yellow, red or blue)

nonstick baking spray, for greasing

1 Pour 200ml (7fl oz) of the cold water into a small bowl and sprinkle over the powdered gelatine.

2 In a saucepan, combine the remaining cold water with 250g (9oz) of the sugar. Stir to dissolve the sugar and bring the mixture to the boil. Boil until the temperature on a sugar thermometer reads 130°C (266°F) – the hardball stage. Remove the pan from heat and whisk in the citric acid and the gelatine mixture until fully dissolved.

3 If you would like to make Gumdrops of different colours and flavours, separate the mixture into the required number of different bowls at this stage. Mix in the flavourings and colourings of your choice, then pour each batch of the mixture into silicone gumdrop moulds in the shape and size of your choice, sprayed with nonstick baking spray. If you have more than one batch of colours and flavours, once the first batch is moulded, reheat the next batch over a very low heat to pour it into the moulds. Leave to set, either at room temperature or in the refrigerator, for at least 1 hour.

4 Remove the sweets from the moulds and roll the gumdrops in the remaining sugar to coat. Store in an airtight container.

Wine gums are a basic food group in my family. My Mum would always have a packet of these firm, chewy sweets in her bag and, when I'm travelling, I always pick up a packet to keep me amused on my journey! Although these sweets are popular worldwide, Britain is home to the Maynard's brand. During the 20th century, Maynard's owned a large chain of sweetie shops and my Nan used to work in one. When she was ready to leave the company, she called up Mr Maynard and told him a secret about one of the shop workers. He told her, 'I can't thank you enough! You can manage any shop in London you want,' but my Nan replied, 'No thanks, I'm tired of standing on my feet!' She left with a lifetime's worth of sweets and many happy memories.

PREP TIME:
5 minutes

TOTAL TIME:
25 minutes,
plus 1 hour for setting

MAKES: 20–30

WiNe gumS

225ml (8fl oz) water

20g (¾oz) powdered gelatine

250g (9oz) granulated sugar

¼ tsp citric acid

6–10 drops of food colouring (you'll need 3–5 drops per colour – try yellow, orange, pink, green or black)

1 tsp flavouring (you'll need ½ tsp per flavour – try lemon, orange, strawberry, mint or anise)

nonstick baking spray, for greasing

1 Put 125ml (4fl oz) of the water in a small bowl and sprinkle over the gelatine.

2 In a small saucepan, combine the remaining water with the sugar. Bring to the boil and continue to boil until the temperature on a sugar thermometer reads 130ºC (266ºF), the hardball stage. Take off the heat.

3 Whisk in the gelatine mixture until fully dissolved, then stir in the citric acid.

4 If you want to make Wine Gums of various flavours and colours, separate the mixture into the required number of different bowls at this stage. With this quantity of the mixture, 2 batches of colours/flavours works well, so use 3–5 drops of each of 2 colours and ½ teaspoon of each of 2 flavours. Work quickly as the wine gum mixture will set rapidly. Thoroughly mix in the colouring and flavouring, then carefully pour the mixture into silicone sweet moulds in the shape and size of your choice, sprayed with nonstick baking spray.

5 Leave the sweets to set for 1 hour, then remove them from the moulds and store in an airtight container.

How to Make
Treat boxes

Receiving or giving – I'm not sure which I prefer! Many of the recipes in this book cost as little as a bag of sugar to make, but the effort taken to make them is the thing that provides the pleasure – along with the contents, of course! Keeping with this 'made from love' theme, these handmade boxes are incredibly simple to assemble and look fabulous as a gift, end-of-party treat or even at a wedding.

YOU WILL NEED

access to a computer and colour printer ✂ copier paper
✂ craft knife and cutting mat ✂ metal ruler
✂ spray adhesive ✂ piece of card

1 Download the treat box designs opposite from my website (vintagepatisserie.co.uk) and print them out at the size you require. Cut them out carefully using a craft knife, cutting mat and metal ruler.

2 Use spray adhesive to mount the designs on to the card.

3 Cut out the individual boxes using the craft knife, cutting mat and metal ruler. Cut a slit where indicated on each half suit symbol – this will allow you to clip the boxes closed once they are assembled.

4 Use the craft knife to score along the fold lines on each box, then bend the pieces of card at the score marks to assemble the treat boxes, closing each box by sliding the suit symbol halves together.

Edinburgh rock was first made in the 19th century by Alexander Ferguson, who became known as 'Sweetie Sandy'. Alexander learned his confectionery trade in Glasgow and then set up his own business in Edinburgh. His Edinburgh rock was so successful that he retired a very rich man! I remember the first time I was given Edinburgh rock on a family holiday. I was most surprised as it was so distinct from the conventional rock I was used to. Initially taken aback, I soon came around to the soft, crumbly texture, and I've been a fan of this traditional Scottish sweet ever since.

EDINBURGH ROCK

150ml (¼ pint) water

450g (1lb) granulated sugar

¼ tsp cream of tartar

4 drops of food colouring (try red or yellow)

½ tsp flavouring (try strawberry or lemon)

PREP TIME:
10 minutes

TOTAL TIME:
45 minutes,
plus 24 hours for drying

MAKES:
20 pieces

1 Place a silicone mat on top of a nonstick baking sheet and set aside.

2 In a heavy-based saucepan, heat the water and sugar gently until all the sugar has dissolved. Bring the mixture to the boil, then add the cream of tartar. Now remove the sugar crystals that are stuck to the inside of the pan above the bubbling solution (*see* page 17).

3 Boil the mixture until a sugar thermometer inserted into the pan reads 126°C (259°F). Take the pan off the heat and mix in the colouring and flavouring. Pour the mixture on to the silicone-lined baking sheet.

4 Pull the sugar (*see* page 18) for about 10 minutes until it has a creamy, chalky consistency. Work quickly, as the sugar will cool quite fast, so there is a short window during which to pull the sugar before it becomes too stiff.

5 Pull the mixture into a long log shape that is about 1cm (½in) in diameter. Cut it into shorter sticks using scissors. Spread these sticks on a sheet of nonstick baking paper and leave to dry for 24 hours at room temperature.

How to make

CUTE COASTERS

With all of this raucous drinking in progress, you must take steps to protect your fabulous vintage furniture from stains with these very cute coasters!

YOU WILL NEED

access to a computer and colour printer ✄ copier paper ✄ craft knife and cutting mat ✄ metal ruler ✄ spray adhesive ✄ cork sheet that is 3–5mm ($^1/_8$–¼in) thick (these can be found in 20cm (8in) square tiles from DIY shops and online; 1 tile makes 4 coasters) ✄ clear sticky back plastic

1 Download the coaster designs opposite from my website (vintagepatisserie.co.uk) and print them out. Cut them out carefully using a craft knife, cutting mat and metal ruler.

2 Use spray adhesive to mount the designs on to the cork sheet.

3 Cut out the individual coasters using the craft knife, cutting mat and metal ruler.

4 Cover the top of each coaster with sticky back plastic to make it waterproof. Make sure that you apply the plastic smoothly and that there are no bubbles beneath it.

5 Trim off any excess plastic to give a neat finish.

SOFT-CRACK & HARD-CRACK SWEETS

There's nothing more satisfying than crunching on a piece of Seaside Rock, or winning a who-can-suck-their-Cola-Cube-the-longest competition! So now you've honed your sweetie-making skills, it's time to embark upon the golden years of your sacred union with sugar! This chapter gives you the tools you need to transform sugar into magnificent hard childhood sweets. This is a gloriously geeky process that involves pulling sugar – a fun, tactile process that requires a healthy amount of physical labour. When you've mastered the art of manipulating the amazing metamorphosis of sugar to 'crack', you'll be able to make such delights as Rhubarb & Custard sweets, Nougat, Toffee, Buttered Brazils, Nut Brittle, Brandy Balls, Cola Cubes, Cough Candy, Sherbet Dip Lollipops, Rose Lollipops and Seaside Rock. Your friends and family won't believe you've made them! But they'll certainly enjoy them, along with the desserts and cocktails inspired by them. So pull out your toffee hammer and prepare to fight tooth and nail for the largest piece!

PREP TIME:
15 minutes

TOTAL TIME:
1½ hours, plus
1–2 hours for setting

MAKES:
about 80 pieces

Instantly recognizable from its Jekyll and Hyde appearance (half rhubarb goodness, half wicked custard), this hard sweetie leads you directly down memory lane. I'm quite confident that someone finishing off their Sunday roast one day with rhubarb and custard pudding simply never wanted it to end – and one of the most famous British sweets was born!

RHUBARB & CUSTARDS

450g (1lb) granulated sugar

150ml (¼ pint) water

½ tsp cream of tartar

1 tbsp liquid glucose

2 tsp citric acid

1 vanilla pod

3–5 drops of red food colouring

caster sugar, for dusting

1 Preheat the oven to 120°C/fan 100°C/gas mark ½ or set up a heat lamp over one end of a silicone mat. Put the granulated sugar, water, cream of tartar and liquid glucose in a saucepan over a medium heat and heat until the sugar is dissolved, stirring gently.

2 When the mixture comes to the boil, remove the sugar crystals that are stuck to the inside of the pan above the bubbling solution (*see* page 17). Keep the mixture bubbling vigorously, without stirring, until it reaches 143°C (290°F) – the soft-crack stage. Then take the pan off the heat and stir in the citric acid.

3 To make the 'custard', scrape the seeds from the vanilla pod on to your silicone mat, then pour half the syrup over them. Set the saucepan over a low heat to keep the remaining mixture syrupy.

4 Pull the sugar (*see* page 18) for about 10 minutes until the candy has a glossy, creamy texture. Work quickly, as the sugar will cool quite fast, so there is a short window during which to pull the sugar before it becomes too stiff. When the candy has the desired texture, put it into the oven or under the heat lamp until you have worked the 'rhubarb'.

5 To make the 'rhubarb', pour the remaining sugar syrup on to the silicone mat. Leave to cool for 10–15 minutes until it is cool enough to pick up. Add the food colouring to the sugar and repeat step 4.

6 Take the 'custard' from the oven or from under the heat lamp and roll both colours into cylinders roughly the same diameter and length. Place one on top of the other and roll them into a single cylinder.

7 Now it's time to make your sweets! Stretch out the candy cylinder until it reaches the desired thickness. Now cut it into 2.5cm (1in) lengths using strong kitchen scissors. Shape the sweets as desired, then roll them in caster sugar while still warm. Allow to set for 1–2 hours. Store in an airtight container.

For as long as I can remember, my Dad allowed me to have advocaat with lemonade at Christmas. It was called a Snowball. We never seemed to finish the bottle and, come January (which also happens to be the start of the rhubarb season), the advocaat would be put back into hibernation. This cocktail gives you a great excuse to use up the rest! Look out for the shocking pink rhubarb crop that can only be found early in the year. The syrup will really raise your spirits and is the perfect palate-cleansing partner for the creamy advocaat.

RHUBARB & CUSTARD COCKTAIL

FOR THE RHUBARB SYRUP

2–3 stalks of rhubarb, cut into 1cm (½in) pieces

200g (7oz) granulated sugar

200ml (⅓ pint) water

FOR THE COCKTAIL

100ml (3½fl oz) rhubarb syrup (see above)

45ml (1½fl oz) brandy

45ml (1½fl oz) advocaat

Rhubarb & Custard sweets (*see page 94*) to serve (optional)

PREP TIME:
10 minutes, plus
20 minutes for cooling

TOTAL TIME:
35 minutes

MAKES: 2

1 To make the rhubarb syrup, put the rhubarb into a saucepan. Add the sugar and water and bring to the boil over a medium heat, then simmer for 5 minutes or until the rhubarb is mushy and tender.

2 Mash the rhubarb with a fork or potato masher. Strain the syrup into a bowl and set this aside to cool completely. Discard the rhubarb pulp – or eat it on ice cream!

3 To make the cocktail, mix the rhubarb syrup and brandy together, then add the advocaat. Pour the drink into 2 glasses and serve with some Rhubarb & Custard sweets, if liked – bloody lovely!

Nougat, made using sugar or honey and nuts, originated in Montélimar in France, during the 17th century, but the Brits have since adopted this tempting, sticky sweet. It has always been my Nan's favourite and we give her some every Christmas as a gift. Until recently I had never made my own but, now I have, there is no going back! Below, I offer three flavour combinations – use only one for this quantity of nougat. So you'll have to make this recipe at least three times to decide which version you like best!

NOUGAT

PREP TIME:
10 minutes

TOTAL TIME:
40 minutes,
plus 3 hours for setting

MAKES: about
18 squares

4 sheets of rice paper
560g (1lb 4½oz) granulated sugar
75ml (2½fl oz) water
500g (1lb 2oz) glucose syrup
2 free-range egg whites,
at room temperature

FOR HAZELNUT NOUGAT
150g (5½oz) toasted hazelnuts
1 tsp vanilla essence

FOR PISTACHIO NOUGAT
100g (3½oz) toasted pistachios
1 tsp rose essence
3 drops of green food colouring

FOR BLUEBERRY NOUGAT
100g (3½oz) toasted almonds
100g (3½oz) dried blueberries
3 drops of purple food colouring

1 You'll need an 18 × 28cm (7 × 11in) baking sheet that has a lip. Line this with nonstick baking paper, allowing it to overhang the sides. Lay 2 sheets of rice paper side by side on a clean work surface. Use the base of the tray as a guide to cut an 18 × 28cm (7 × 11in) rectangle using the 2 sheets (as 1 is likely to be too small). Repeat with the remaining 2 sheets. Position 2 sheets of the paper in the base of the lined tray.

2 Place the sugar and water into a saucepan. Use a wet spoon to spoon the glucose syrup into the pan and set the pan over a medium-low heat. Stir the contents with a wooden spoon, brushing down the sides of the pan occasionally with a pastry brush dipped in warm water, until the sugar dissolves.

3 Now place a sugar thermometer into the saucepan in which you are making the syrup. Increase the heat to high and bring the mixture to the boil. Reduce the heat to medium-high and boil, uncovered and without stirring, until the temperature of the syrup reaches 120°C (248°F). At this point, it's time to prepare the egg whites (the sugar syrup should continue to cook). Put the egg whites into the clean, dry bowl of a food mixer. Use the whisk attachment to whisk the egg whites until firm peaks form. Alternatively, use a hand mixer to whisk the eggs.

4 When the sugar reaches 150°C (302°F), immediately remove the pan from the heat. Set the food mixer with the beaten eggs still in the bowl on a medium speed

and slowly pour the hot syrup into the egg whites in a thin, steady stream. Don't pour the syrup down the sides of the bowl or on to the whisk as it may set before being incorporated into the egg whites. Once all the syrup is incorporated, whisk the mixture for a further 3 minutes or until thick and glossy.

5 Use a wooden spoon to mix your chosen combination of nuts, flavouring and colouring into the egg white mixture until well combined. Work quickly or the nougat will begin to set. Also, ensure the nuts and flavouring are at room temperature – if they are cold, the mixture will set too rapidly, making it difficult to transfer to the baking sheet.

6 Quickly pour the nougat evenly into the lined baking sheet using a spatula to scrape down the sides of the bowl. Use the spatula or the back of a spoon dipped in hot water to spread the nougat evenly across the baking sheet and smooth the surface. Place the remaining rice paper over the top of the nougat and press down gently. Set aside in a cool, dry place for 3 hours or until set.

7 Lift the nougat from the baking sheet using the overhanging baking paper and place it on a cutting board. Remove the baking paper. Use a serrated knife in a sawing motion to cut the nougat into pieces that fit your box, or place the nougat in a clean, dry airtight container, separating layers with nonstick baking paper. Keep in a cool, dry place for 1–2 weeks or in the refrigerator for up to 3 weeks. If you are storing the nougat in the refrigerator, bring it to room temperature before you serve it.

Once you have made your Nougat you can easily take a few more steps to make this delicious Nougat Affogato. With bitter espresso, sweet nougat and optional liqueur, this is the perfect way to satisfy the tastebuds after dinner.

Nougat Affogato

PREP TIME:
10 minutes

TOTAL TIME:
10 minutes

MAKES: 3

3 scoops of vanilla ice cream

100g (3½oz) nougat of your choice (*see* pages 98–101), cut into small pieces

3 double espressos (approximately 60ml/2¼fl oz per shot)

135ml (4½fl oz) Kahlua Coffee Liqueur (optional)

1 Place the ice cream in 3 bowls and sprinkle each with the nougat pieces.

2 Pour a double espresso over the top of each dessert, followed by a third (45ml/1½fl oz) of the Kahlua, if using. Serve immediately.

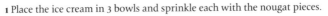

How To Make a
NOUGAT BOX

During my Nan's employment at Maynard's (a very famous 20th-century sweet-shop chain in London), nougat came in a blue box. My Nan remembers nothing else apart from it being blue, so this is my take on what I would have hoped it looked like. Use a light card for the best effect.

YOU WILL NEED

access to a computer and colour printer ✄ copier paper ✄ spray adhesive ✄ white card (3 × A4 sheets per box) ✄ craft knife and cutting mat ✄ ruler ✄ glue stick ✄ florists' cellophane

1 Download the decorated templates for the box lid (shown opposite), box base and separator insert from my website (vintagepatisserie.co.uk) and print them out. Spray the back of each printed sheet with adhesive and mount it on to a sheet of card. Leave to dry.

2 Once the glue is completely dry, use the craft knife, cutting mat and ruler to neatly cut out the lid and the base. Next, cut out the hole in the lid.

3 Fold in the sides of both pieces, folding along the dotted lines. Now glue the tabs on the base to the flaps to secure them in place and repeat this process for the lid to make your two-piece box.

4 Cut a square of florists' cellophane that is 1cm (½in) larger than the hole in the box lid. Use the glue stick to attach the cellophane square to the inside of the lid, ensuring that the hole is neatly covered.

5 To make the separator insert, mount the printout of the insert on to card and cut out each of the pieces, as before. Now slot the shorter pieces into the marked slots on the two longer pieces to complete the insert, and place it inside the box.

cut-out section
for cellophane

Last year, my partner Dick gave me a Blue Bird toffee hammer as a gift for my birthday. It's a gorgeous thing, and toffee hammers are connected with some lovely family history for me. My late father-in-law, George, always carried around a tin and hammer and, every time he got a new tin of toffee, his seven children (and Mum) would partake in a slab-breaking ceremony. Every piece of the broken toffee slab would be of a different size, so you can imagine the family politics involved in choosing a piece to eat! This recipe is dedicated to George for keeping this long-forgotten family tradition alive.

Toffee Slab

PREP TIME:
10 minutes

TOTAL TIME:
30 minutes, plus
2 hours for setting

MAKES: enough for
6–8 people

FOR THE TOFFEE

500g (1lb 2oz) granulated sugar

125g (4½oz) unsalted butter

125ml (4fl oz) golden syrup

125ml (4fl oz) water

FOR THE TOPPING
(OPTIONAL)

200g (7oz) dark or milk chocolate

125g (4½oz) chopped almonds

1 You'll need a baking sheet that's roughly 30 × 43cm (12 × 17in) and has a lip around the edges. Line this with nonstick baking paper.

2 Place all the toffee ingredients in a saucepan over a medium heat. Stir until the sugar has dissolved, bringing the mixture to the boil. Once it comes to the boil, stop stirring and remove the sugar crystals that are stuck to the inside of the pan above the bubbling solution (*see page 17*).

3 Now place a sugar thermometer into the saucepan. Boil the toffee until the temperature on a sugar thermometer reaches 150°C (302°F), then pour it into the lined baking sheet. Leave the toffee to set for 1 hour.

4 If you are making the topping, break the chocolate into pieces and melt it in a heatproof bowl set over a saucepan of barely simmering water, making sure that the base of the bowl doesn't touch the water. Remove the melted chocolate from the heat and pour it over the top of the set toffee slab. Sprinkle with the chopped almonds and leave to set for 1 hour. Once the toffee has set, smash it into pieces with a toffee hammer.

When you're making the Toffee Slab (*see* opposite), why not make a couple of separate pieces? Then once the toffee-breaking ceremony is over, you and your partner can put the kids to bed and enjoy this fruity, sharp-tasting cocktail.

'THE TOFFEE APPLE'

crushed ice

50ml (2fl oz) apple brandy

300ml (½ pint) cloudy apple juice

2 toffee discs that are about the size of a £2 coin, made by following the Toffee Slab recipe (*see* opposite) and dripping the molten toffee mixture on to a greased marble slab to achieve discs of the correct size

PREP TIME:
5 minutes

TOTAL TIME:
5 minutes

MAKES: 2

1 Pop the crushed ice, apple brandy and cloudy apple juice into a cocktail shaker and shake.

2 Pour the drink into 2 cocktail glasses and, just before serving, pop a toffee disc into each glass.

Toffee slab

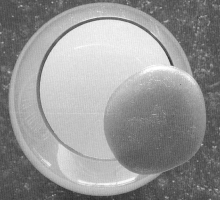

'The Toffee Apple'

Buttered Brazils are one of my Granny's favourites and are often referred to as 'the Rolls Royce of sweets'. These whole brazil nuts wrapped in a blanket of creamy butterscotch really are a true British classic. They are rich and sumptuous and, to enhance the effect, you can even buy metallic gold papers to wrap them in. My senses are excited just by unwrapping them!

PREP TIME:
10 minutes

TOTAL TIME:
35 minutes, plus
30 minutes for setting

MAKES:
200g (7oz)

Buttered Brazils

325g (11½oz) caster sugar

125ml (4fl oz) water

2 tbsp golden syrup

25g (1oz) butter

200g (7oz) brazil nuts

1 Line a baking sheet with nonstick baking paper. Combine the sugar, water, syrup and butter in large heavy-based saucepan. Stir over a medium heat, without boiling, until the sugar is dissolved.

2 Once the sugar dissolves, bring the mixture to the boil and boil for about 20 minutes or until it reaches 150ºC (302ºF) – at this stage, the hot toffee should be the colour of caramel and a teaspoonful of the mixture will set and crack if dropped into a cup of cold water.

3 Remove the pan from the heat and, when the bubbles subside, add the nuts, 4–5 at a time. If you add too many, the toffee will cool too fast and will set before you get a chance to take the nuts out. Working quickly, using silicone or greased tongs or 2 forks, lift out the nuts, one at a time, and place them on the prepared baking sheet. Leave them to set at room temperature, which will take about 30 minutes.

I love making truffles on a regular basis as gifts for friends and family – it astonishes me how expensive (and stale-tasting!) shop-bought truffles can be. The making process is incredibly quick and simple – using chopped Buttered Brazils (*see* opposite) gives a fantastic texture, and there is plenty of fun to be had (so expect lots of mess)! Truffles will keep for a couple of weeks in the refrigerator, but take them out a few hours before serving because they taste best at room temperature. You'll find the ideal packaging suggestion for these delicacies on pages 84–5.

BUTTERED BRAZIL TRUFFLES

PREP TIME:
10 minutes

TOTAL TIME:
15 minutes, plus
3 hours for setting

MAKES: 24

275g (9¾oz) dark chocolate, broken into pieces

60g (2¼oz) unsalted butter, at room temperature

250ml (9fl oz) double cream

1 quantity Buttered Brazils (*see* opposite), whizzed in a food processor until they have the consistency of breadcrumbs

1 Place the chocolate and butter in a large bowl. In a saucepan, bring the cream to the boil, then pour it over the chocolate and butter. Stir the mixture gently until the chocolate has melted.

2 Leave the mixture to cool for 2 minutes, then stir in half the processed Buttered Brazils. Now place the truffle mixture in the refrigerator for a minimum of 3 hours. For the best results, leave it in the refrigerator overnight.

3 Place the remaining processed Buttered Brazils in a dish. Divide the set truffle mixture into 24 pieces and roll each of these into a ball. Now roll each ball in the chopped nuts to coat.

Buttered Brazil Truffles

Buttered Brazils

This one is a real crowd-pleaser, no matter if you're six or 60, nobody can resist that satisfying crack as the Nut Brittle caramel is broken. Whenever I make this for friends and family, there's always a battle to see who gets to bring down the hammer. Inevitably, one of the youngsters wins, leaving the adults feeling secretly jealous! I like to use walnuts, hazelnuts or almonds or, even better, a mixture of all three. This treat is at its best the first few days after making, so crack it at a party to add a little excitement, then wrap the remaining brittle in pretty bags to be taken home as gifts.

PREP TIME:
10 minutes

TOTAL TIME:
35 minutes, plus
30 minutes for setting

MAKES: 15 pieces
of varying size

Nut Brittle

300g (10½oz) whole walnuts, hazelnuts, almonds
or a mixture of all three
250g (9oz) granulated sugar
½ tsp salt

1 Preheat the oven to 140ºC/fan 120ºC/gas mark 1.

2 Scatter the nuts on to a baking sheet, then toast them for 6–10 minutes or until golden – don't let them burn. Allow them to cool slightly but, while they are still warm, rub off the skins using a tea towel.

3 Line a baking sheet with nonstick baking paper.

4 Tip the sugar into a heavy-based, wide nonstick saucepan, add a splash of water and heat gently (do not stir) until the sugar has dissolved.

5 Now place a sugar thermometer into the saucepan and continue heating the sugar until it reaches a temperature of 150ºC (302ºF) – at this stage, the sugar will have an even light brown colour all over. Now take it a step further to a slightly deeper brown, watching the mixture carefully so it doesn't burn.

6 Scatter in the salt, then the toasted whole nuts and shake the pan so the nuts become well coated in the caramel.

7 Quickly and carefully pour the mixture on to the prepared baking sheet. Allow it to cool completely, so it sets and hardens (about 30 minutes), then break the brittle into pieces with a hammer, ready to eat or to wrap as gifts.

Brandy balls have been in production since 1877. These amber gems are one of our most treasured old-fashioned sweets. Originally made for the Christmas season, they give a feeling of festive warmth. I think they are too nice to be enjoyed just once a year and should be eaten all year round! Made using real brandy, they will warm your cockles and turn your cheeks a rosy shade of red.

PREP TIME:
20 minutes

TOTAL TIME:
1¾ hours,
plus 1 hour for drying

MAKES:
about 40

BRANDy balls

nonstick baking spray, for greasing (optional)

450g (1lb) granulated sugar

150ml (¼ pint) brandy

½ tsp cream of tartar

1 tbsp liquid glucose

½ tsp brandy essence (optional)

icing sugar, for coating

1 First prepare your sweet moulds. You will need more than 1 mould for the quantity given – remember that each sweet is made from two hemispheres. Either use silicone hemisphere sweet moulds sprayed with nonstick baking spray or, if you are feeling adventurous, make your own (*see* page 17). Next, preheat the oven to 110°C/fan 90°C/gas mark ¼.

2 Put the sugar, brandy, cream of tartar and liquid glucose into an ovenproof pan and heat gently until the sugar is dissolved, stirring gently. When the mixture comes to the boil, remove the sugar crystals that are stuck to the inside of the pan above the bubbling solution (*see* page 17).

3 Keep the mixture bubbling vigorously, without stirring, until it reaches 154°C (310°F). Take the pan off the heat and stir in the brandy essence, if liked. Pour half the mixture into a heatproof bowl, then transfer the pan with the remaining half to the oven to keep it warm while you fill the sweet moulds with the mixture from the bowl using a piston funnel (*see* page 17 for how to improvise one), a Pyrex jug or simply a spoon – but be wary of drips.

4 When you have made the first batch of sweet halves, allow them to cool completely, which will take about 30 minutes, then pop them out of the moulds and leave them, flat side down, on a sheet of nonstick baking paper. Make the second batch in the same way.

5 When the second batch is in the moulds but still slightly liquid, pop one of the hemispheres from the first batch on top of one of the hemispheres in the second batch to construct a ball. Repeat with the remaining hemispheres from the first and second batches. Leave to set for 20–30 minutes. Repeat this process until you have used up all the sweet mixture. Once set, roll the brandy balls in icing sugar. Store the sweets in an airtight container.

As far back as the Middle Ages, sugar has been combined with medicine to 'sweeten the pill', and since the beginning of the 20th century, a whole array of lozenges, gums and pastilles have served as throat soothers. I remember as a child exaggerating even the smallest cough so that my Mum would give me a soothing sugary throat sweet to ease my symptoms. Sucking on one of these fiery aniseed treats would always banish my imaginary sore throat.

COUGH CANDY

PREP TIME:
15 minutes

TOTAL TIME:
1¼ hours,
plus 1 hour for setting

MAKES:
about 80

350g (12oz) granulated sugar

100g (3½oz) liquid glucose

¼ tsp cream of tartar

100ml (3½fl oz) water

½ tsp anise extract (or use clove extract)

3–5 drops of orange food colouring

50g (1¾oz) icing sugar mixed with 50g (1¾oz) caster sugar

1 Preheat the oven to 110°/fan 90°C/gas mark ¼ or set up a heat lamp over one end of a silicone mat. Place a large saucepan over a low heat and add the sugar, liquid glucose, cream of tartar and water. Stir slowly until the sugar is completely dissolved. Then remove the sugar crystals that are stuck to the inside of the pan above the bubbling solution (see page 17).

2 Increase the heat to medium-high and bring the mixture to a hard boil. Then, without stirring, bring the syrup to 154°C (310°F). Remove the pan from the heat and place it in a large, iced water-filled bowl for 30 seconds to flash cool the pan and arrest cooking.

3 Pour the syrup on to the silicone mat and let it rest for 1–2 minutes to cool some more. Then add the anise or clove extract and the food colouring.

4 Pull the sugar (see page 18) for about 10 minutes until the candy has a glossy, creamy texture. Work quickly, as the sugar will cool quite fast, so there is a short window during which to pull the sugar before it becomes too stiff. When the candy has a glossy, creamy texture, put it under the heat lamp to soften for about 5 minutes.

5 Cut off 2 equal-sized pieces of your candy and roll them into thin sausages. Lay them side by side and twist them into 1 piece. Cut to length using strong kitchen scissors, then toss in the icing sugar-caster sugar mixture to coat. Leave to set for at least 1 hour. If you like, you can wrap the sweeties individually in baking paper for a pretty presentation. Store in an airtight container.

COUGH CANDY

BROWN BROS
SUPERIOR
CONFECTIONERY
2 OZ 1 D
Cross Skelton St
COLNE.

Now I'm a little older, I still exaggerate my coughs and colds from time to time, but nowadays it's to persuade my partner to make me a more grown-up version of my fond Cough Candy childhood memory. With spicy King's Ginger liqueur and soothing lemon and honey, this cocktail goes down a treat, whether you're feeling a little under the weather or not!

COUGH CANDY TODDY

PREP TIME:
5 minutes

TOTAL TIME:
10 minutes

MAKES: 1

1 breakfast tea bag
250ml (9fl oz) hot water
45ml (1½fl oz) King's Ginger liqueur
50ml (2fl oz) fresh orange juice
honey, to taste (optional)
1 slice of lemon
1 Cough Candy sweet (*see* page 116), crushed

1 Put the tea bag in a teacup and add the hot water. Now add the King's Ginger, orange juice and honey, if liked.

2 Skewer the lemon slice on to half a kebab stick.

3 Remove the tea bag from the drink.

4 Rest the skewered lemon slice on top of the teacup. Sprinkle the crushed Cough Candy sweet on the lemon slice and serve.

How To Make
Teacup Cosies

When serving up the Cough Candy Toddy (*see* page 118) to your guests, you can add style to even the most unattractive cups by making leather teacup cosies with bright contrasting buttons. These will allow you all to get cosy wrapping your hands around your hot drinks without fear of burning your mitts.

YOU WILL NEED

approximately 25cm (10in) black leather ✂ a teacup with straight sides ✂
tailor's chalk or pale coloured pencil ✂ ruler ✂ 5p piece ✂
fabric scissors ✂ craft knife and cutting mat ✂ needle ✂ black thread
✂ round orange buttons (3 per teacup cosy)

1 Draw the shape of the teacup cosy on the back of the leather. To do this, lay the leather on a work surface, wrong side facing up. Place the teacup on top on its side with the handle facing towards you. Place the tailor's chalk by the rim of the cup and roll the cup away from you and, at the same time, follow the rim with the chalk. Roll the cup back and repeat the same movement along the bottom of the cup, drawing a second line.

2 You now have two long lines running parallel to each other on the leather. Join these up to form a rectanglular shape: using a ruler, draw a straight line from the end point of one of the lines to the corresponding end point of the other to join them. Next join the end points at the other end of the shape, but this time, draw a scalloped line using a 5p piece as a guide to make the curves neat. Cut out the shape with fabric scissors.

3 Wrap your leather piece around your teacup and mark a line with the tailors' chalk where you need to cut a slit for the handle. Draw a narrow rectangle in this position that is just wide enough to comfortably fit the teacup handle through. Now cut out the rectangle carefully using the craft knife and cutting board.

4 Cut three small slits along the scalloped edge of the leather for the buttonholes. They need to be just big enough to push your buttons through.

5 Sew three buttons along the straight edge of the leather to correspond with the positions of the buttonholes at the other end of the teacup cosy.

6 Wrap the cosy around the cup and fasten the buttons. Check it fits neatly and trim off any edges that are not flush.

I was quite shocked, when researching this book, to discover that cola cubes are not actually made using cola! I had to tell my brother, as this was always his favourite sweet when we were growing up (they often filled his pockets) and, as a consequence, I always think of cola cubes as a bit of a boys' sweet. I would feel quite grown up and privileged when my big brother allowed me to have one! Images of him in the 1980s playing with a Rubik's Cube in the garden, shoving red sugary cubes into his mouth, will always remain a vivid childhood memory.

PREP TIME:
15 minutes

TOTAL TIME:
1¼ hours, plus 1–2 hours for setting

MAKES: 40

Cola Cubes

nonstick baking spray,
for greasing (optional)

450g (1lb) granulated sugar

150ml (¼ pint) water

½ tsp cream of tartar

1 tbsp liquid glucose

½ tsp vanilla extract

½ tsp lemon extract

½ tsp orange extract

¼ tsp cinnamon extract

½ tsp citric acid

about 5 drops of red
food colouring

icing sugar, to coat

1 First prepare your sweet moulds. You will need more than 1 mould for the quantity given, or you can work in batches. Either use silicone ice-cube trays sprayed with nonstick baking spray or, if you are feeling adventurous, make your own (*see* page 17).

2 Put the granulated sugar, water, cream of tartar and liquid glucose into a saucepan over a low heat and heat it until the sugar is dissolved, stirring slowly.

3 When the mixture comes to the boil, remove the sugar crystals that are stuck to the inside of the pan above the bubbling solution (*see* page 17).

4 Keep the mixture bubbling vigorously, without stirring, until it reaches 154°C (310°F) – the hard-crack stage. Take the pan off the heat and allow the mixture to cool to approximately 110°C (230°F), then stir in the flavourings, citric acid and colouring.

5 Fill the sweet moulds with the mixture using a piston funnel (*see* page 17 for how to improvise one), a Pyrex jug or simply a spoon – but be wary of drips. Leave for 1–2 hours until completely cool.

6 Pop the sweets out of the ice cube trays as you would ice cubes. If taking them out of an icing sugar mould, simply pick them out. Roll the cubes in icing sugar (to stop them from sticking to one another) and store them in an airtight container.

Sarsaparilla is a soft drink originally made from the *Smilax regelii* plant. As with the Cola Cube (see page 122) this drink also inspired a hard sweet and, although I do not hold memories of this, my partner and father have many – enough memories, in fact, to inspire hours of discussion! The Sarsaparilla drink was famous in Hollywood Westerns between the 1930s and 1950s, at which time an order of this beverage at the bar would be met by much mockery from the manly cowboys nearby! This cocktail is defiantly dedicated to them!

Sarsaparilla cocktail

PREP TIME:
1 hour, plus 1 hour
for cooling

TOTAL TIME:
2 hours 5 minutes

MAKES: 2

FOR THE CONCENTRATE

3 tbsp sarsaparilla root

1 stick of liquorice root (they tend to come in lengths of approximately 10cm/4in)

1 litre (1¾ pints) water

450g (1lb) granulated sugar

FOR THE COCKTAIL

50ml (2fl oz) concentrate (*see* left)

50ml (2fl oz) tequila

150ml (¼ pint) sparkling water

ice cubes

2 sticks of liquorice root, to decorate

1 To make the concentrate, mix the sarsaparilla, liquorice root and water in a large saucepan and simmer for about 45 minutes without boiling the mixture (boiling it at this stage can make it become bitter).

2 Add the sugar, then bring the mixture to the boil and continue to boil for 5 minutes.

3 Strain the mixture into a clean pan, then place it over a high heat and simmer for an additional 5 minutes until it has a syrupy consistency.

4 Transfer the mixture to a bowl or jug and chill it in the refrigerator for about 1 hour until cold. (You can leave it in the refrigerator until you're ready to make and serve the drink.)

5 When you're ready to make the cocktail, mix the concentrate, tequila and sparkling water in a cocktail shaker and pour it into 2 glasses over ice. Serve immediately with sticks of liquorice root as stirrers.

How to Make
Cocktail Monkeys

If your cocktail tastes fabulous but is lacking in visual appeal, these simple monkey cocktail pendants will give everyone that cheeky grin. Say bye bye 1980s umbrellas and hello monkey! Making them can be a little fiddly, but as long as your guests don't take them home, they can be used again and again. Try to print them on the thickest card possible before waterproofing them. We don't want Mr Monkey getting drunk!

YOU WILL NEED

access to a computer and colour printer ✄ copier paper ✄
spray adhesive ✄ thick white card ✄ paper scissors ✄
clear sticky back plastic

1 Download the two monkey pendant designs and their mirror images opposite from my website (vintagepatisserie.co.uk) and print them out, then use the spray adhesive to mount your colour print-outs on to card.

2 Cut out the designs neatly, then glue the matching pairs (one front piece, one back piece) together so that the same monkey design is on both sides.

3 Cover both sides of each cocktail monkey with sticky back plastic. Now cut out the monkeys, leaving a 1mm (1/32in) edge of plastic around each monkey to create a waterproof seal and make the pendant more long-lasting.

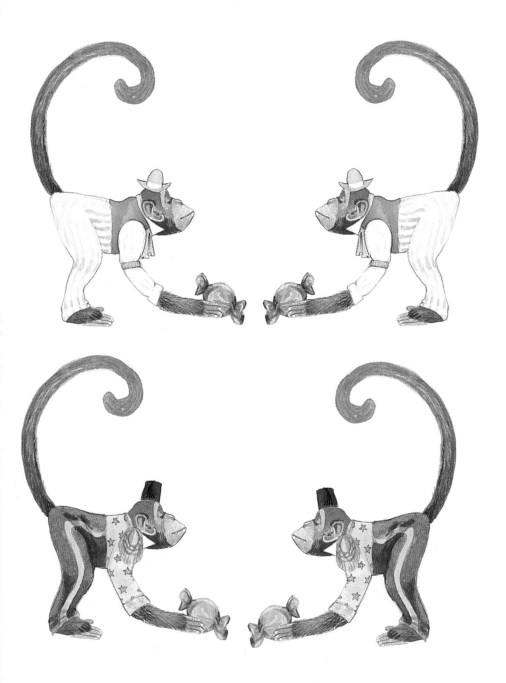

Sweet lollies and sharp sherbet – Sherbet Dip Dabs had flavour as well as longevity. I often bought this sweet because it would sometimes last for up to an hour, if I could resist the temptation of biting the lolly. Sherbet dips are great for kiddies' parties. Making your own allows you to add any flavour to either the sherbet or the lolly, and to choose your favourite colours, or colours that are suited to the theme of the party.

SHERBET DIP LOLLIPOPS

PREP TIME:
15 minutes

TOTAL TIME:
40 minutes, plus
1 hour for setting

MAKES: 15

FOR THE SHERBET
300g (10½oz) icing sugar
2 tsp citric acid
1 tsp bicarbonate of soda
¼ tsp lemon flavouring

FOR THE LOLLIPOPS
4 tbsp water
1 tbsp glucose syrup
225g (8oz) caster sugar
4–5 drops of the food colouring of your choice
¼ tsp flavouring of your choice (try vanilla, mint, lemon, orange or almond)

1 Line a silicone mat or baking sheet with nonstick baking paper, then chill in the freezer – you need it to be very cold.

2 To make the sherbet, place the dry ingredients into the bowl of a food mixer and mix for 5 minutes on the slowest setting, dripping in the lemon flavouring slowly during the mixing period. Set aside.

3 For the lollipops, put the water, glucose syrup and caster sugar into a small saucepan and bring to the boil over a medium-high heat. When the mixture comes to the boil, it's time to get rid of the sugar crystals on the inside of the pan above the bubbling solution (see page 17). Continue to boil the mixture

until it reaches 154ºC (310ºF) – the hard crack stage. Once it does, remove the pan from the heat and stir in the colouring and flavouring of your choice.

4 Remove the chilled silicone mat or baking sheet from the freezer and set it on your work surface. Lay out 15 lollipop sticks across the mat or sheet, then pour spoonfuls of the sugar syrup mixture over and around the sticks to form the traditional disc shape. Don't worry if the shapes aren't perfectly round – they'll still look lovely! Leave the lollies to cool completely, then wrap them individually – with a spoonful of sherbet – in florists' cellophane or baking paper tied with string or sticky tape. Alternatively, insert each into a Sherbet Dip Bag (see pages 132–3).

Once upon a time, the only way to get the jazz in a drink was to add some sherbet! I like old-fashioned rituals, so if you have leftovers after making your Sherbet Dip Lollipops (*see* opposite), why not crack out the gin and enjoy a fizz sensation?!

Gin Fizz

FOR THE SUGAR SYRUP

100g (3½oz) granulated sugar

100ml (3½fl oz) water

FOR THE COCKTAIL

45ml (1½fl oz) gin

50ml (2fl oz) sugar syrup (*see* above)

50ml (2fl oz) lemon juice

90ml (3fl oz) sparkling water

2 Sherbet Dip Lollipops, together with some sherbet (*see* opposite)

PREP TIME:
10 minutes,
plus 20 minutes
for cooling

TOTAL TIME:
35 minutes

MAKES: 2

1 For the sugar syrup, mix the sugar with the water in a small saucepan. Bring to the boil, then turn off the heat and leave to cool completely.

2 Once the sugar syrup is cool, you can mix the cocktail. Combine the gin, sugar syrup and lemon juice in a jug. Pour the mixture into 2 glasses and top up each one with half the sparkling water. Decorate with a Sherbet Dip Lollipop sprinkled with some sherbet. Just prior to drinking, stir in the sherbet with the lolly and enjoy!

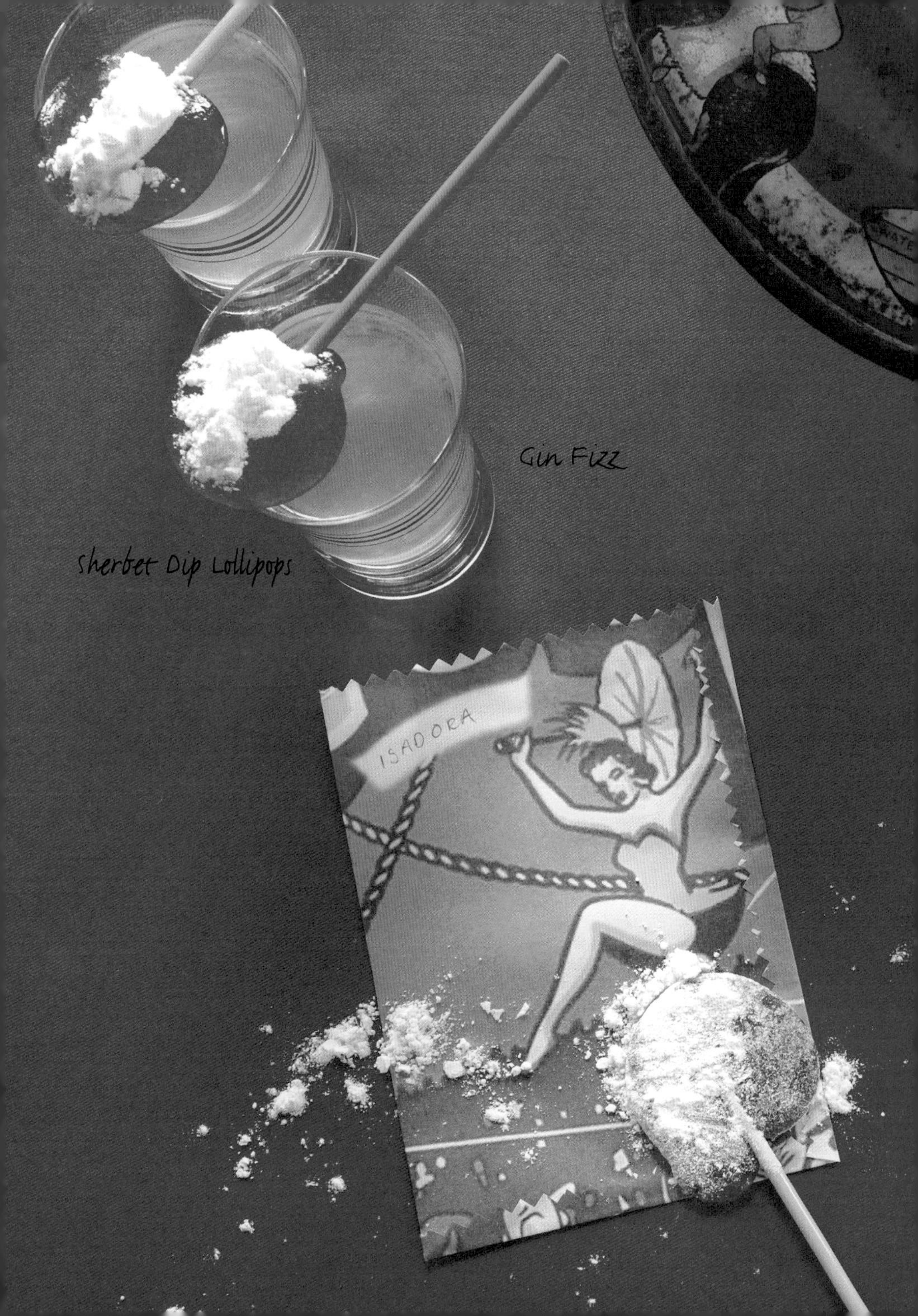
Gin Fizz
Sherbet Dip Lollipops
ISADORA

sherbet Dip Bags

How to Make
SHERBET DIP BAGS

Paying attention to the details and making your guests feel how special they are will elevate any party. This simple yet very cute paper bag provides a lovely way of handing out sweets at the end of your party. Stationed at the door in your vintage party dress, equipped with a boxful of funky paper bags, each name-tagged and brimming with delectable sweeties, you will have everyone wondering how you find the time. No one will know the bags are done in just half an hour!

YOU WILL NEED

access to a computer and colour printer
✄ A4 white copier paper (1 sheet per bag)
✄ pencil ✄ ruler ✄ paper scissors ✄
pinking shears ✄ glue stick

1 Search online to find some images you would like to use on your bags, then print them out on white A4 paper. Your images need to fill an entire page, so you may have to resize them.

2 Use a pencil and ruler to measure and copy the bag template opposite on to the back of each sheet of paper, then cut it out. Use pinking shears to cut along the edges shown with a zigzag line on the template. This will help to create a traditional sweetie-bag look.

3 Now fold along the dotted line.

4 Glue down the zigzag flaps to finish your bag. Then simply repeat for as a many bags as you wish to make.

This would not be an Angel Adoree book if I did not dedicate something new entirely to the rose. Sweets conjure memories and make us feel nostalgic. With this in mind, I'm hoping this Rose Lollipop will give you feelings of sweet floral delight and start new memories for some.

Rose Lollipops

nonstick baking spray, for greasing

225g (8oz) granulated sugar

100ml (3½fl oz) glucose syrup

60ml (2¼fl oz) water

2 tsp rose water

4 drops of pink or red food colouring

¼ tsp powdered white food colouring (optional)

PREP TIME:
5 minutes

TOTAL TIME:
20 minutes,
plus 30 minutes
for setting

MAKES: 8

1 Lightly spray a rose-shaped silicone lollipop mould with nonstick baking spray. Insert a lollipop stick into each of the recesses in the mould.

2 Combine the sugar, glucose syrup and water in a saucepan over a medium-high heat. Stir until the sugar dissolves. When the mixture comes to the boil, remove the sugar crystals that are stuck to the inside of the pan above the bubbling solution (*see* page 17). Insert a sugar thermometer and allow the mixture to boil, without stirring, until it reaches 154°C (310°F) – the hard-crack stage.

3 Remove the mixture from the heat. Allow it to sit until it stops bubbling. Then add the rose water and food colouring and stir until they are evenly dispersed. (If you'd like to make opaque lollipops, add a drop or two of white food colouring when you add the pink or red colouring.)

4 Fill the recesses in the lollipop mould until you run out of the mixture. Ensure the lollipop sticks are well embedded.

5 Allow the lollipops to cool for 30 minutes at room temperature before removing them from the moulds. Wrap the lollipops individually in florists' cellophane or baking paper tied with string or sticky tape then store in an airtight container at room temperature for up to a month.

Inspired by my recent holiday to Morocco, this Rose Lollipop Cocktail is very distinct in flavour. The cardamom is quite powerful, but if you like this flavour combination you may have found your new favourite drink. Dipping your Rose Lollipop is a great way to avoid getting drunk too quickly (hiccup!).

Rose Lollipop Cocktail

PREP TIME:
5 minutes

TOTAL TIME:
10 minutes

MAKES: 2

1 cardamom pod

50ml (2fl oz) rose syrup

1 tbsp lemon juice

2 tbsp orange juice

50ml (2fl oz) gin

crushed ice

150ml (¼ pint) sparkling water

2 Rose Lollipops (*see* page 135)

1 Grind the cardamom pod into fine pieces in a mortar with a pestle.

2 Combine the rose syrup, lemon juice, orange juice, gin and cardamom in a cocktail shaker. Add the ice and shake.

3 Strain the mixture into 2 cocktail glasses and top up each glass with the sparkling water. Decorate each glass with a Rose Lollipop and serve.

I'd be surprised if I met any Brit that doesn't have a childhood memory of seaside rock. Mine is of being at a Blackpool funfair, where I wanted to buy gifts for my best friend. I was mesmerised by the variety of colours and was pleasantly surprised by how reasonably priced a piece of rock was! (Yep, even at the age of six, I appreciated value for money!) It's easy to buy rock when in the UK or on the internet, but the pleasure, fun and achievement of making your own can't be purchased anywhere.

PREP TIME: 5 minutes

TOTAL TIME: 1½ hours, plus 1 hour for setting

MAKES: 20 pieces

ᴐ Seaside Rock ᴐ

450g (1lb) granulated sugar

275g (9¾oz) glucose syrup

250ml (9fl oz) water

15 drops of food colouring (use 5 drops each of yellow, red and green)

1½ tsp flavouring (use ½ tsp each of lemon, strawberry and mint)

1 Preheat the oven to 110°C/fan 90°C/gas mark ¼. Line a large baking sheet with a sheet of nonstick silicone baking paper.

2 Put the sugar, glucose syrup and water into a large saucepan set over a medium-high heat and stir to dissolve the sugar completely. Bring the mixture to the boil, then remove the sugar crystals that are stuck to the inside of the pan above the bubbling solution (see page 17).

3 Boil the mixture until the temperature reaches 154°C (310°F) – the hard-crack stage. Remove the pan from the heat and pour one-third of the mixture on to a silicone mat. Halve the remaining mixture, placing each half in its own saucepan. Add the yellow colouring and lemon flavouring to the portion on the mat. Add the red colouring and strawberry flavouring to the second portion, and the green colouring and mint flavouring to the third portion. Set the two saucepans over a low heat to keep the remaining mixture syrupy.

4 Working one portion at a time, pull the sugar (see page 18) for about 15 minutes until the candy has a glossy, satiny texture. Work quickly, as the sugar will cool quite fast, so there is a short window during which to pull the sugar before it becomes too stiff. If the mixture becomes too hard when pulling, warm it in the oven for 5 minutes on the prepared baking tray to soften it. If you have a heat lamp, place the mass under the heat lamp for 5 minutes instead.

5 Now it's time to make your rock! Roll all 3 colours into cylinders of roughly the same diameter and length. Place all 3 on top of one another and roll them into a single cylinder, twisting as required. Cut the rock into lengths of your choosing. Allow to cool completely then store in an airtight container.

The hard work is in the making of Seaside Rock (*see* page 139), so what better way to celebrate your worthy endeavours than with a gingery Rocktail? Never one to resist a pun, I would add this tasty drink to the party menu on the basis of name alone!

PREP TIME:
5 minutes

TOTAL TIME:
5 minutes

MAKES: 2

ROCKTaiL

a few pieces of Seaside Rock (*see* page 139)
100ml (3½fl oz) King's Ginger liqueur
300ml (½ pint) lemonade
150ml (¼ pint) ginger beer
crushed ice

1 Place a few pieces of Seaside Rock in the bottom of each cocktail glass.

2 In a cocktail shaker, combine the liqueur with the lemonade, ginger beer and crushed ice. Stir well, then pour the mixture into the cocktail glasses over the pieces of Seaside Rock and serve immediately.

The machine-spun version of candy floss we are all familiar with today was the result of an unusual partnership between a dentist and a confectioner back in 1897. When you're a child, there's something truly magical about candy floss – that feeling of butterflies you get in your tummy as you approach a funfair; the sight of children dashing around brandishing pink fluffy clouds; young couples sharing a stick of candy floss to sweeten their stroll. Well now you can recreate the magic yourself!

candy floss

nonstick baking spray, for greasing

75ml (2½fl oz) cold water

100ml (3½oz) golden syrup

400g (14oz) granulated sugar

4 drops of the food colouring of your choice (optional)

PREP TIME:
35 minutes

TOTAL TIME:
1½ hours

MAKES:
6 large portions

1 Cut the curving tops off a balloon whisk using a pair of heavy-duty wire cutters. You'll be left with a circle of spikes. Spread these out until there is roughly a 1cm (½in) space between each spike. Wash the doctored balloon whisk and dry it thoroughly. Next, take 6 pieces of A4 paper and roll each piece into a narrow cone, then secure each cone with sticky tape. These cones are the 'sticks' that will hold your candy floss.

2 Spray the handles of 2 wooden spoons or spatulas with nonstick baking spray. Position these about 20cm (8in) apart on the edge of your work surface so that the handles extend over the edge of the counter and the bowls of the spoons remain on the counter. Place a heavy weight over the bowl of each wooden spoon on the work surface, to hold the spoon in place. Arrange a large plastic sheet (an opened-up bin bag will do) over the floor under the spoon handles.

3 Put the water, syrup and sugar into a saucepan over a medium heat and stir until the sugar dissolves. Keep the mixture bubbling vigorously, without stirring,

until it reaches 160°C (320°F). Remove it from the heat, pour it into a Pyrex bowl and stir in your selected food colouring, if liked.

4 Dip the cut ends of your doctored whisk into the sugar, then lift it about 10cm (4in) above the surface of the liquid. When the sugary drips stop falling, wave the whisk from side to side rapidly, above the spoon handles, moving it a couple of feet beyond each handle (depending on the size of your plastic sheet). Allow the sugar strands (or 'floss') to fall on to the spoon handles.

5 When you have a mass of candy floss resting on your spoon handles, and before it sets completely, collect it up by rolling it around the open end of the paper cone while rotating the cone (the strands will stick together). Repeat the process with the remaining sugar syrup and paper cones to form 6 portions of candy floss. Alternatively, place the candy floss on to tall cocktail glasses and serve with the Fairground Fancy (see page 145).

How to Make
Organza Pom-Poms

Capture the magical essence of candy floss and bring it to your party by decorating with these easy-to-make pom-poms. They make a wonderful statement as your guests enter a room and are bound to bring a little funfair excitement to your celebration.

YOU WILL NEED

newspaper (about 1 sheet per small pom-pom) ✀ kitchen foil ✀ several metres (yards) of thin ribbon (about 2m/6½ft per small pom-pom) ✀ fabric scissors ✀ needle with a large eye ✀ pint glass (to use as a template – anything circular will do, but a pint glass is a good size) ✀ several metres (yards) of organza or other thin fabric in a few colours (about 1m/3ft per small pom-pom) ✀ tailor's chalk ✀ lots of pins (you may use a few hundred)

1 Make the centre of your pom-pom by scrunching up newspaper into a ball – try to make it as round as possible. Then cover it with kitchen foil to give it some structure.

2 Cut a length of ribbon that's twice the length you want the hanging loop of your pom-pom to be. Thread the needle with the ribbon, push it into the ball at any point, then push it out about 2.5cm (1in) further up the ball. Thread the ribbon through the ball, leaving a short length of ribbon free at the point of entry. Tie the part of the ribbon that emerges from the ball to the end of the ribbon where it enters the ball, making a loop.

3 Use the open end of the pint glass as a template and draw around it on the organza using tailor's chalk to create lots of circles (15 circles would be enough for a small pom-pom). Now cut out your circles. (You may wish to fold the fabric over several times before drawing the circles so you are cutting through several layers at once to save time, as you will need lots of circles to create a good effect.)

4 Take a circle and fold it in half, then into quarters. Push a pin through the folded corner at the centre of the circle, then into the foil ball. It will hold firm in the ball and the fabric will fan out a little. Repeat this process until the whole ball is covered, spacing the circles roughly 3cm (1¼in) apart.

5 When your pom-pom looks full and fluffy, it can be hung anywhere you desire using the ribbon you attached earlier.

Candy floss isn't just for the kids! For those of you with a sweet tooth, this cocktail with crème de cassis, lemon juice and real candy floss (*see* the picture on page 142) will disappear even quicker than the sweet itself.

♪Fairground Fancy

2 × 25g (1oz) balls of Candy Floss (*see* page 143 – use about ¼ of a regular portion per ball)

45ml (1½fl oz) fresh lemon juice or bitter lemon

45ml (1½fl oz) crème de cassis

45ml (1½fl oz) vodka of any flavour

ice cubes

100ml (3½fl oz) sparkling water

PREP TIME:
3 minutes

TOTAL TIME:
8 minutes

MAKES: 2

1 Take 2 tall cocktail glasses and place a ball of Candy Floss inside each.

2 Shake the juice or bitter lemon, crème de cassis and vodka together in a cocktail shaker with the ice cubes.

3 Strain the mixture into the glasses over the Candy Floss. Top up with sparkling water and serve immediately.

HOW TO MAKE
HARLEQUIN PUPPET
BUNTING

Inspired by the original jointed paper dolls produced by Pellerin printmakers in Épinal, France, our harlequin couple will elevate your Sweet-Tea Party with colourful vibrancy. Use as bunting, puppets or hanging dolls – you will never want to put up polka-dot bunting again!

YOU WILL NEED

Access to a computer and colour printer ✄
A4 copier paper ✄ paper scissors ✄ glue stick

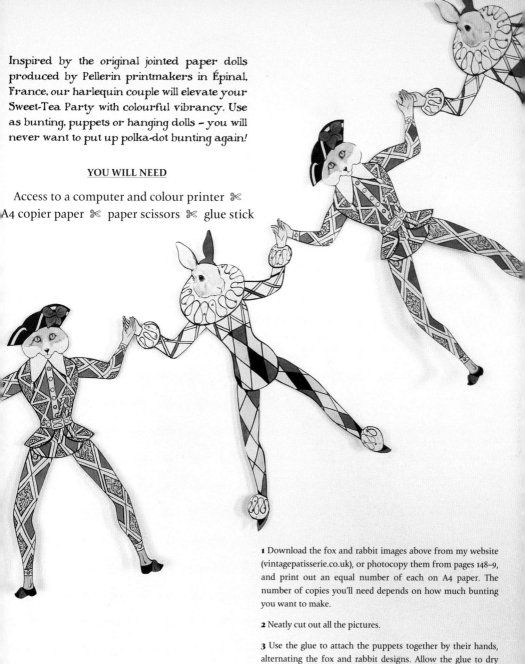

1 Download the fox and rabbit images above from my website (vintagepatisserie.co.uk), or photocopy them from pages 148–9, and print out an equal number of each on A4 paper. The number of copies you'll need depends on how much bunting you want to make.

2 Neatly cut out all the pictures.

3 Use the glue to attach the puppets together by their hands, alternating the fox and rabbit designs. Allow the glue to dry thoroughly before hanging your bunting.

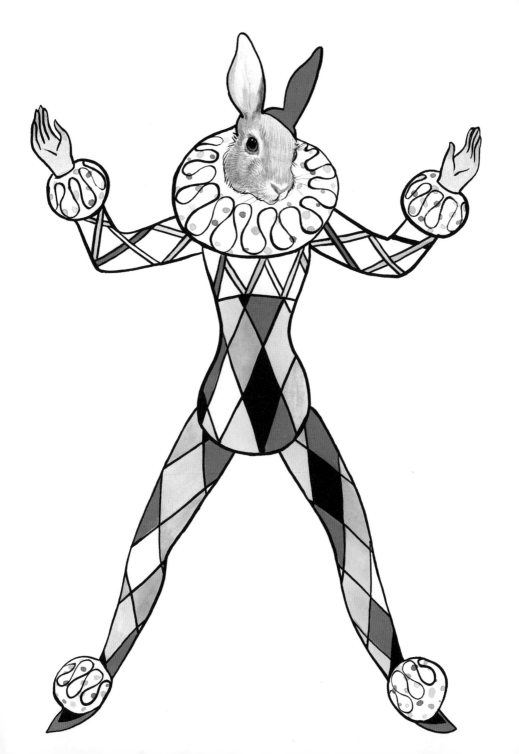

~ How to Make
HARLEQUIN PUPPETS

If you fancy something interactive for the children, you can use the same characters used to make the bunting to create these Harlequin Puppets (*see pages 152–3*). Kids will have endless fun with them and they double up as a stylish bedroom decoration! I sometimes even make a few puppets in various sizes and have them on show dangling from the ceiling at Sweet-Tea Party events.

YOU WILL NEED

access to a computer and colour printer ✄ copier paper ✄ spray adhesive ✄ coloured card ✄ paper scissors ✄ gold split pins (8 per puppet) ✄ string ✄ sticky tape ✄ stick (find one that is as straight as possible)

1 Download the images for the fox and rabbit puppet pieces from my website (vintagepatisserie.co.uk), or photocopy them from pages 152–3 and print them out.

2 In a well-ventilated area, spray the backs of the printed sheets with adhesive, then mount each piece on to a sheet of coloured card. Once the adhesive is completely dry, cut out the designs neatly.

3 To enable you to move the puppets' arms and legs, you need to cut them at the elbows and knees. Cut straight across these joints, then round off the newly cut edges.

4 Join the separated parts together at the shoulder, elbow, hip and knee joints using eight split pins per puppet (one split pin per joint).

5 Cut two lengths of string that are roughly 46cm (18in) long (ensuring they are of exactly the same length) and another two lengths that are about 35cm (14in) long (again, ensuring they are of exactly the same length). Attach one end of a long piece of string to the back of one of the puppet's knees using sticky tape, then repeat with the other long piece of string and the other knee. Attach one end of a short piece of string to the back of one of the puppet's elbows, then repeat with the other short piece of string and the other elbow. Then tie the loose ends of all four pieces of string to a stick. By moving the stick you can bring your puppet to life.

Repeat the steps above to make a selection of puppets that can be played with by your Sweet-Tea Party guests or hung up as decorations.

RESOURCES

Making sweeties does not have to be an expensive hobby – equipment and ingredients tend to be reasonably priced and you don't need too many specialist products. Of course, you'll need to procure the odd item now and then as you expand your sweet-making repertoire so that, over time and without a punch to your pocket, you'll build up a useful cache of sweetie-making tools. Make sure that you shop around for the best deals. If you don't have the time, below is a list of specialist items that are called for in some of the recipes in this book, along with details on where to find them in the UK.

Black food colouring paste

I use this for making Liquorice (*see* page 76) and I prefer the Sugarflair brand myself. Search for "Sugarflair black extra paste colour" at www.cakecraftshop.co.uk.

Edible markers

These useful items allow you to inscribe your love on your edible makes – I sometimes use them for writing messages on Love Hearts (*see* pages 44–5). They are often available in specialist kitchen shops and craft suppliers and are easily found on Amazon – search for "edible food markers" or "food pens". The ones I use are from Amazon, listed as "Americolour set 10 food pens".

Flavourings

When making Liquorice (*see* page 76), I use anise extract – search for it by name at www.lakeland.co.uk.

When making Parma Violets (*see* page 36), I use violet flavouring, which I get from www.cake-stuff.com – search for "violet natural flavouring".

Golden light corn syrup

The grocery chain Whole Foods Market carries this product at specific locations in London. If you don't live in the Big Smoke, you can order it online at Ocado or Amazon – search for "corn syrup".

Liquorice root

Search for this product by name on Amazon.

Nonstick baking spray

This highly useful product is often available at the big supermarkets and many local grocery shops. You can find it online at Amazon or Ocado – search for it by name.

Piston/portion funnel

If you don't want to make one of these using an ordinary funnel (*see* page 17), search for "piston funnel" on Amazon or www.nisbets.co.uk.

Rice paper

The sheets of rice paper I use are usually 15.5 × 25.5cm (6 × 10in). These are easily found on eBay, or you could try www.cakecraftshop.co.uk – search for "edible sugar sheets and rice paper".

Sarsparilla root

Search for this product by name on Amazon.

Silicone moulds

For silicone mouse-shaped moulds, which I use to make Sugared Mice (*see* page 24), try www.siliconemoulds.com and search for "mice". They can also be found on eBay or Amazon, or at www.lakeland.co.uk.

For silicone gumdrop moulds, try www.lakeland.co.uk or Amazon as well as specialist kitchen shops.

For rose-shaped silicone lollipop moulds, search for "silicone cake jelly soap mould pan sugarcraft rose decorating tins bakeware" on eBay.

The marketplace www.alibaba.com is a good source for lollipop moulds in a variety of wonderful shapes, such as flowers and stars. Search for "silicone lollipop mould".

I use heart-shaped silicone moulds for making Fudge Hearts (*see* page 48), which are available from Amazon. Search for "silicone heart shaped chocolate mould".

Text-embossing set

Sometimes, when I make Fudge Hearts (*see* page 48), I like to stamp love messages on to them – a lovely touch for special occasions such as Valentine's Day or for when your heart is bursting with emotion that you just must express! If you'd like to do the same, search for "text embossing set" on Amazon.

Tylose powder

You'll need this product if you wish to make edible glue (*see* page 35). Search for it by name on Amazon – you'll find a number of suppliers.

VINTAGE PATISSERIE THANK YOU

Ariotek For being the best web-hosting company I've ever come across. Drew and Colin, you are both amazing! *ariotek.co.uk*

Angeline Francis For meeting and falling in business love! Can't wait to see where this year leads us.

Barnett Lawson Trimmings For being the only haberdashery I'll ever need to go to. London is worth a visit just for you. *www.bltrimmings.com*

Beauty Seen PR Michelle, you are an amazing business woman. Thank you for supporting us, both as a client and as a Revlon sponsor! We adore you! *www.beautyseenpr.com*

Ben Spriggs Ben! Thank you for your support of the previous books and I hope you love this sweet version! *www.thesundaytimes.co.uk*

Benefit Cosmetics For making the "Big Beautiful Eyes" product. *www.benefitcosmetics.com*

Bethan Soanes For being stunning, and for being there for the VP every time we need you! Lovely seeing your career take off!

Beyond Retro For being a one-stop for vintage clothes and accessories, and where most of my wardrobe is from! *www.beyondretro.com*

Birdy Imoke For being all that and a little bit more! *www.londonwestendwi.blogspot.co.uk*

Caroline Alberti I have three books' worth of thank yous to make to you! Thank you for your relentless hard work on these beauties. I honestly don't know how we managed to get this book turned around in time. You are like the Father Christmas of books – a miracle worker! *www.octopusbooks.co.uk*

Carolyn Whitehorne For your support, encouragement and for being a friend. *www.toniandguy.com*

Cass Stainton For understanding me and throwing some pretty amazing parties! I miss you!

Cate Sevilla at Bitch Buzz Darlin', I love your energy, ambition, drive and humour – I'm your number-one FAN! *www.bitchbuzz.com*

Charlotte Crittenden It's been such a pleasure working with you this year!

Cliff Fluet For becoming my friend, for your support, for your encouragement, for understanding what I want to achieve. Cliff, you are amazing. *www.lewissilkin.com*

Company Magazine For your support, always. *www.company.co.uk*

Dandy Dan Dan, you are a true gentleman. I know you work inhouse now, but I'll always hold you to that coffee we talked about!

David Carter For being a loyal, eccentric dandy. Your creativity has no limits. P.S. I think I did sell more books than you? :-) *www.alacarter.com*

Deborah Meaden For believing in me and providing me with a stepping stone to grow my business. I've achieved a lot this year, including welcoming my incredible son Arthur to the world! I hope you will meet him one day! Thank you. *www.deborahmeaden.com*

Denham Broadcast & Digital To Jill, for being a bit mental and for loving Arthur! And to Grace, for believing in me. *www.denhams.tv*

Denise Bates For being so supportive in a tough year. You are an amazing lady! *www.octopusbooks.co.uk*

Eleanor Maxfield For commissioning the first book! For totally getting the second book! For making miracles happen with the third! For being by my side and supporting me every step of the way. You believe, you care and you are always fair. That totally rhymes! So happy you have become my friend. *www.octopusbooks.co.uk*

Elnett Hairspray What would we do without you? *www.loreal-paris.co.uk/styling/elnett.aspx*

Emma Perris For the wonderful massages you give, for your support and for being my mate! *emmaperris.co.uk*

Fleur Britten For being fabulous and supportive. It was lovely seeing you become a beautiful mum! *www.fleurbritten.moonfruit.com*

Fleur de Guerre For being a gorgeously talented ghetto vintage lady. For jumping in when I have needed you and for being a good friend. Please stop being so fabulous. *www.diaryofavintagegirl.com*

Fraser Doherty and Anthony McGinley For being business inspirations. I'm always so proud to say you are my friends! *www.superjam.co.uk*

Grazia For your support. *www.graziadaily.co.uk*

Harpers Bazaar For your support. *www.harpersbazaar.com*

Hazel Holtham For being an amazing business woman and friend. Hazel, you are a beauty inside and out, and it's been a joy watching your business develop and even more of a joy to watch you fall in love – I'm actually going to get my hat soon! *www.ragandbow.com*

Hotcake Kitty For being such a hard-working beauty! I'm glad you're on my team! *www.hotcakekitty.com*

John Moore For training me when I was 18, for helping at every step of the way, for caring and being a true friend. *www.rsmtenon.com*

Karen Baker For creating a bible of press that only a person who cares and has drive could achieve! You do the work of an entire team and I could not ask for more. Thank you for being so wonderful. I'm looking forward to "press-ing" this book, just so we get to talk more! *www.octopusbooks.co.uk*

Kathy Garner at Past Perfect For having a brilliant company that sells amazing music! *www.pastperfect.com*

Katie, Poppy and Richard For being the first to make a real business out of vintage – you are the leader, OH KATIE! For being my friend and inspiring me. Thanks for your support. Let's take over the world! ;-) *www.whatkatiedid.com*

Lady Luck For being the first vintage dance club in London and for being so fabulous. *www.ladyluckclub.co.uk*

Laura Ashley For being a fabulous client with a fabulous team and brand. *www.lauraashley.com*

Laura Cherry For being such a beauty, inside and out. You are an inspiring lady, hard working, and I'm proud that you are achieving your dream. Thank you for being part of the team.

Lauren Craig For caring where your flowers come from, for being so talented and for being my friend. *www.thinkingflowers.org.uk*

Leanne Bryan Thank you for caring and for being so gentle and calming. I could not ask for more from an editor! *www.octopusbooks.co.uk*

Lian Hirst For having the best fashion PR label in town. Thank you for your support and for being an amazing friend. You have totally spoilt me and Arthur this year. We are so lucky and I'm looking forward to repaying the favour at your fabulous wedding! *www.tracepublicity.com*

Lipstick & Curls For your inspiring hairstyles and for being amazingly talented. Thank you for your support and for being my friend and letting your whole family be in this book! *www.lipstickandcurls.net*

M·A·C Cosmetics For creating the perfect look. What would a girl do without her Ruby Woo? *www.maccosmetics.com*

Margaret at Vintage Heaven Margaret! You are the most amazing woman that roams the planet! Your positivity fills my heart. In fact, Dick is quite sure it's changed our lives. We truly love you! You have spoilt us this year – thank you for being such a caring friend. *vintageheaven.co.uk*

Martin Miller's Gin The only gin to use! Thank you for your support on the last book launch! I'm so in love with this gin! *www.martinmillersgin.com*

Mehmet at Simply Fresh I'm so proud of you!

Miranda Keyes We found you by chance but it was meant to be! Thank you for being such a great food stylist and for being so organized! Nothing was too much trouble and I can't thank you enough for being part of this book. *www.miranda-keyes.com*

Naomi Thompson For your support and love of vintage! *www.naomithompson.co.uk*

Nina Butkovich-Budden Oh Nina! Leader of the vintage hair pack! You are so talented. I miss you! *ninashairparlour.com*

Octopus Publishing Group team For all being so lovely and for believing in this book! *www.octopusbooks.co.uk*

Patrick at Value My Stuff For being inspiring and having such a great business. *www.valuemystuff.com*

Peter and Sasha For always bringing amazing life to every party! I wish I could have you more!

Pete Katsiaounis For doing the illustrations for all my websites! You go beyond the call of duty. *www.inkandmanners.com*

Rob Davies For having an amazing business and being a friend! Your energy and support always makes me smile. Thank you. *www.tracepublicity.com*

Rokit Thank you for being the first vintage shop I ever bought anything in! Imogen Excell, they are lucky to have you and so is Pandora! *www.rokit.co.uk*

Rosie Alia Johnson For being a beautiful spirit and part of the team. For bringing the first clothes collection to life – it will happen! And for making such lovely hair flowers! You are a very talented beauty. *www.rosiealia.blogspot.co.uk*

Sales at Octopus Beccs, Kevin, Siobhan, Terry, Vanessa (listed in alphabetical order)… Sales! Thank you for getting the book out into the big wide world! You do me proud and I know you talk about the book with passion. Thank you! *www.octopusbooks.co.uk*

Salima Hirani For understanding my voice and making it flow. Thank you. I'm now on your diet, so when I loose my baby weight I'm taking you out for cake. *www.giraffebooks.com*

Sarah Keen For being so bloody supportive and brilliant at everything you do! I've loved watching your taxidermy classes grow and I've loved working with you and having you as my crafty Girl Friday on this book. Vintage weddings next – your wedding, maybe?! Xx *www.curiousmenagerie.co.uk*

Sharon Trickett For being incredibly hard-working and talented and utterly fabulous. It's been lovely watching you grow Minnie Moons. *www.minniemoons.com*

Simone Hadfield Where does one start?! Thank you for throwing yourself into the Vintage Patisserie and investing your heart! It's been brilliant watching your journey as entrepreneur and I'm looking forward to seeing you grow. I know you will get everything you wish for. *www.miss-turnstiles.blogspot.co.uk*

Sophia Hunt, Belladonna Beauty Parlour Thank you for creating my fabulous hair for the front cover! I'm so proud and so happy you were part of the day and your beauty graces the front cover! You are an incredibly talented lady and I wish you luck in whatever your future holds.

Sophie Laurimore For being a very supportive agent! For understanding my life. It's been great growing our businesses together. Thank you to you and your family for being so fabulous and for being on the front cover! *www.factualmanagement.com*

Stylist For your support. *www.stylist.co.uk*

Suck and Chew For having the best sweet shop in East London. Vicki and MJ, you are a wonderful business couple and wonderful neighbours! *www.suckandchew.co.uk*

Susie and the Luna & Curious team Susie. Your creativity inspires me. You must see this in everything I do now. Thank you for bringing the Luna & Curious people together and for your 24/7 support! *www.lunaandcurious.com*

Time Out London For your continued support. *www.timeout.com/london*

Top Shelf Jazz Always there to perform a treat! Thank you for always being amazing at everything I have booked you for. *www.topshelfjazz.com*

Uncle Roy's For selling edible flowers (roses) and having the most fabulous company! *www.uncleroys.com*

Vintage Victory G & K – how do you get to be so wonderful in your field and be parents?! I take my vintage hat off to you. *www.vintagevictory.com*

Yasia Williams-Leedham For so much, I don't even know where to begin. Firstly, for your dedication and hard work. For your love of every project. For understanding what I want in your sleep! I don't think I could work with anyone else – well, want to, for sure! Your insight and advice as a working mum has been incredible. I love you YW! *www.octopusbooks.co.uk*

Yuki Sugiura For caring and for being so talented and creative. Work is not meant to be this fun! You understand exactly what makes my mind work and, together, we are a great team. Your food photography makes me smile like a Cheshire cat. *www.yukisugiura.com*

I haven't met you, but I want to thank you for inspiring me and exciting me and being a layer of who I am today:

Her Majesty the Queen, Louise Brooks, Clara Bow, Greta Garbo, Bette Davis, Mae West, Vivien Leigh, Ava Gardner, Rita Hayworth, Ginger Rogers, Betty Grable, Lewis Carroll, Charles Worth, Gabrielle 'Coco' Chanel, Madeleine Vionnet, Elsa Schiaparelli, Christian Dior, Billie Holiday, Ella Fitzgerald, Doris Day, Sammy Davis Jnr (thank you for 'Mr Bojangles'), Nina Simone, René Gruau, Minnie Ripperton, Bill Withers, Curtis Mayfield, Stevie Wonder, Michael Jackson, Prince, Vivienne Westwood and Alexander McQueen.

ANGEL ADOREE THANK YOU ♡

Adele Mildred The year of the wedding! The year of becoming a full-time genius! It's your year! And I'm glad I'm here by your side as your friend. Thank you for being such a wonderful, fabulous friend. I love you.

Alison Coward Thank you for being so proud and supporting me every step of the way.

Andreya Triana Thank you for filling my life with music and love and endless praise! If I could sing, I'd ask for a voice like yours.

Bobby Nicholls and Lord Ian You finally made it into the book, you busy boys! My best party boys! I just need to party more! Which now needs planning! Please can we make this happen?

Christina Lau I always feel very emotional when I need to express my thank yous to you. Your love and continued belief in me, teaching me how to bake, helping with websites, business problems and, now, endless mum advice… you are my friend and my mentor and one of the few people I can turn to for help. I now have a new level of appreciation for everything you have done, as you did lots as a new mum! I love you darlin'.

Darren Whelen My oldest friend. Thank you for your love and support and for reminding me to stop every now and again! Congratulations on your new life! I'm so happy for you. I need to meet Princess Nahla.

David Edwards You are my dearest friend, the perfect gentleman and a creative wizard. I can't wait to be your half Best Man at your wedding this year! Thank you for your endless support and stunning photography. I love you!

Elizabeth Osbourne Thank you for caring and teaching me to read! Your memory has never been forgotten.

Fred and Katja Künzi For taking me out of London and giving me the best memories I could wish for.

Gaia Facchini (Mouthful O' Jam) You slipped into our lives and it's like you were always here. Thank you.

Gary Nurse What a pleasure it's been seeing you be a sensational father. I'm so proud of you. Thank you for your friendship, support and knowing me well enough to always have a right answer in a crisis! Not only are you a beautiful man to look at, the beauty goes much deeper and I love you so much for this.

Gossica Anichebe For making me laugh, and for your love and friendship. Thank you.

Grandma and Grandad You are dream grandparents and I'm so lucky to have you both. Your love for your extending family knows no bounds and I can't wait until Arthur Donald gets to know his namesake and finds out how wonderful his great grandparents are.

Jim Walker Arthur's gorgeous "non-religious" Godfather! Thank you for being so friggin' wonderful and managing to be in London for everything special this year! We are very lucky to have you in our lives and have been so spoilt by you and David. I can't wait for Arthur to get to know you and see your beauty inside and out. I love you.

John, Julie and Katie Walker My second family! Thank you for the love I receive all the way from over the pond! Not to mention taking me around all the vintage shops every time I come to visit!

Joseph Yianna For friendship and support and for being so fabulous!

Judith Biffiger For sharing your world, inspiring me with music and love and being the gentlest, sweetness person ever!

Kate and Joe Skully For making me laugh until my sides split, for being bloody fabulous and for the love and support you have always shown. You finally made it into the book! Front cover only, darlin'!

LeaLea Jones For singing like an angel, for your open heart and for knowing that hard work pays off. Ms Jones, you are an inspiration to me and your peers around you. Hackney is a lucky place.

Leah Prentice For being the second Vintage Patisserie team member! And for being my mate and causing me to laugh too many times. Mwah!

Lee Behan Life's a pitch and I'll never forget it! Thank you for being inspiring and supportive!

Leo Chadburn I'll always remember how we met. I was sitting in a bar with my feet on the table and you approached me and said "your shoes are fabulous, would you like to party?" I'm not quite sure if that's how it happened, but that's what I'll go with. Fourteen years of friendship later and I love you so much. Your mum was proud of what an amazing son she has.

Mel Patel For being my mate and the only DJ I'd ever employ.

Mum and Dad I've always thanked you for the years I remember, but I have a new appreciation now for all the years I don't remember! You are wonderful parents and amazing grandparents. I can see the way you look at Arthur and know that's how you looked at me – unconditional love. I'm the person I am because of you both. I know you tell me how proud you are of me, but I am of you both, too.

Nan For being you, Nan – I love you.

Natasha For your love and support.

Paul For being a great brother and a great dad! I'm looking forward to Arthur getting to know his Uncle Paul. You are a kid at heart and that's why kids fall in love with you!

Sarah, Leroy, Henry and Oscar The panda dress is yours! Thank you for going beyond the call of friendship and believing in me. In your own words, I can't wait for our families to grow up together. Thank you for being there and holding my hand!!!

Seymour Nurse When I see your name, I smile. Your kind words live in my heart and I'll love you forever Peter Pan!

Taj Cambridge Every year feels as if we have achieved a lifetime of dreams. I see us both take steps on our journey every day, but we will never get to the end because we want to pack our lives to the brim with tales and experiences. I'm loving our journey. I love you.

Tate and Anthony You two lovebirds are so inspiring with your business ventures! I love being around you and learning new stuff! www.anytodo.com is genius and that's purely because of you both.

The Strawbridges It's worrying that I feel so at home with you because you are all wonderfully crazy! I could not feel more loved and it's magical to see us grow as a family. Arthur is so loved, he may just pop. I love you all.

Val and Co at the Palm Tree For giving me the best nights of my life and for being such a lovely family!

Vicki, Young, Rosy and Theo For your love and support, and for the party years! I've loved seeing your family grow and I can't wait for our families to grow up together. Thank you for being so generous on every level. I love you all.

INDEX